Exploring **C**anada

ALBERTA

Titles in the Exploring Canada series include:

British Columbia

Manitoba

Ontario

Quebec

Yukon Territory

Exploring Canada

ALBERTA

by Gordon D. Laws and
Lauren M. Laws

**LUCENT
BOOKS ®**

THOMSON

GALE

San Diego • Detroit • New York • San Francisco • Cleveland • New Haven, Conn. • Waterville, Maine • London • Munich

Development, management, design, and composition by Pre-Press Company, Inc.

LIBRARY OF CONGRESS CATALOGING-IN-PUBLICATION DATA

Laws, Gordon D.
 Alberta / by Gordon D. Laws and Lauren M. Laws.
  v. cm. — (Exploring Canada series)
Includes bibliographical references and index.
Contents: The Princess Province — Prairies, parklands, mountains, and forests —
The fur trade and the First Nations — Settling the West — Life in Alberta today —
Arts and culture — Facing the future — Facts about Alberta.
 ISBN 1-59018-045-3 (hardback : alk. paper)
 1. Alberta—Juvenile literature. 2. Alberta—History—Juvenile literature.
[1. Alberta. 2. Canada.] I. Laws, Lauren M. II. Title. III.
Series.
 F1076.4 .L39 2003
 971.23—dc21

Printed in the United States of America

Contents

Foreword

Any truly accurate portrait of Canada would have to be painted in sharp contrasts, for this is a long-inhabited but only recently settled land. It is a vast and expansive region peopled by a predominantly urban population. Canada is also a nation of natives and immigrants that, as its prime minister Lester Pearson remarked in the late 1960s, has "not yet found a Canadian soul except in time of war." Perhaps it is in these very contrasts that this elusive national identity is waiting to be found.

Canada as an inhabited place is among the oldest in the Western Hemisphere, having accepted prehistoric migrants more than eleven thousand years ago after they crossed a land bridge where the Bering Strait now separates Alaska from Siberia. Canada is also the site of the New World's earliest European settlement, L'Anse aux Meadows on the northern tip of Newfoundland Island. A band of Vikings lived there briefly some five hundred years before Columbus reached the West Indies in 1492.

Yet as a nation Canada is still a relative youngster on the world scene. It gained its independence almost a century after the American Revolution and half a century after the wave of nationalist uprisings in South America. Canada did not include Newfoundland until 1949 and could not amend its own constitution without approval from the British Parliament until 1982. "The Sleeping Giant," as Canada is sometimes known, came within a whisker of losing a province in 1995, when the people of Quebec narrowly voted down an independence referendum. In 1999 Canada carved out a new territory, Nunavut, which has a population equal to that of Key West, Florida, spread over an area the size of Alaska and California combined.

As the second largest country in the world (after Russia), the land itself is also famously diverse. British Columbia's "Pocket Desert" near the town of Osoyoos is the northernmost desert in North America. A few hundred miles away, in Alberta's Banff National Park, one can walk on the Columbia Icefields, the largest nonpolar ice cap in the world. In parts of Manitoba and the Yukon glacially created sand dunes creep slowly across the landscape. Quebec and Ontario have so many lakes in the boundless north that tens of thousands remain unnamed.

One can only marvel at a place where the contrasts range from the profound (the first medical use of insulin) to the mundane (the invention of Trivial Pursuit); the sublime (the poetry of Ontario-born Robertson Davies) to the ridiculous (the comic antics of Ontario-born Jim Carrey); the British (ever-so-quaint Victoria) to the French (Montreal, the world's second-largest French-speaking city); and the environmental (Greenpeace was founded in Vancouver) to the industrial (refuse from nickel mining near Sudbury, Ontario, left a landscape so barren that American astronauts used it to train for their moon walks).

Given these contrasts and conflicts, can this national experiment known as Canada survive? Or to put it another way, what is it that unites as Canadians the elderly Inuit woman selling native crafts in the Yukon; the millionaire businessman-turned-restaurateur recently emigrated from Hong Kong to Vancouver; the mixed-French (Métis) teenager living in a rural settlement in Manitoba; the cosmopolitan French-speaking professor of archaeology in Quebec City; and the raw-boned Nova Scotia fisherman struggling to make a living? These are questions only Canadians can answer, and perhaps will have to face for many decades.

A true portrait of Canada cannot, therefore, be provided by a brief essay, any more than a snapshot captures the entire life of a centenarian. But the Exploring Canada series can offer an illuminating overview of individual provinces and territories. Each book smartly summarizes an area's geography, history, arts and culture, daily life, and contemporary issues. Read individually or as a series, they show that what Canadians undeniably have in common is a shared heritage as people who came, whether in past millennia or last year, to a land with a difficult climate and a challenging geography, yet somehow survived and worked with one another to form a vibrant whole.

The Princess Province

Named for a daughter of Queen Victoria, Alberta has been called the princess province. It has also been dubbed the Cinderella province for its surprising transformation from an overlooked distant relative to a suddenly wealthy and popular figure, one capable even of inspiring jealousy. For some, Alberta is merely a stodgy prairie province. Still others see Alberta as the place where the wild west still lives, where freewheeling entrepreneurs, ranchers, and farmers tame the land and manipulate its resources for their benefit.

There is some truth to all of these views. Though it is the site of two of the largest cities in Canada, much of Alberta remains rough and untamed, and there are parts where few people if any make their homes and struggle for their livelihoods. Throughout the province, the varied Alberta landscape challenges the people and shapes their characters. In the far north, where the vegetation is thin and the land may thaw only briefly during the summer, a tough breed of miners and drillers makes their living cut off from much of the outside world. On the prairies, even when crop prices are high, drought, fire, insects, and other threats may easily wipe out months and years of effort. Still, modern farmers manage to make the land some of the most productive in the world.

Alberta's two huge cities, Edmonton and Calgary—both almost one million strong—are the true symbols of Alberta's rise to national power in Canada. Edmonton was begun as a

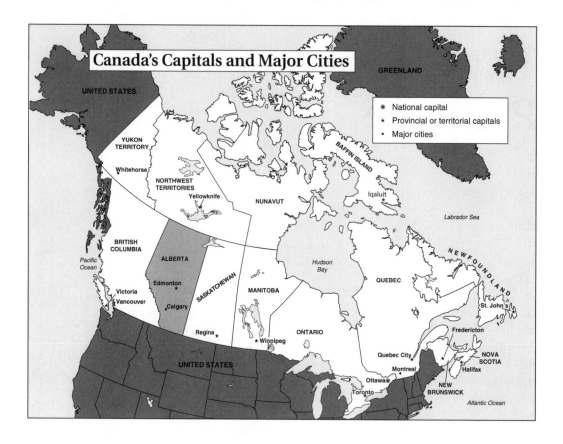

Canada's Capitals and Major Cities

fur trading post in the late eighteenth century. Calgary was a recently built Northwest Mounted Police fort when Canadian government officials decided to run the country's first transcontinental railway through it in the 1880s. What the two cities have in common are close links to the energy boom of the past fifty years, thanks to the province's considerable reserves of oil, natural gas, and coal.

Alberta's recent energy boom and the explosive growth of Edmonton and Calgary have caused, according to some observers, a fundamental shift within Canada, moving political and economic strength away from the east and turning cities like Quebec into mere regional powers when they had previously enjoyed national prominence. Even in sports, the power of Edmonton's and Calgary's ice-skating and hockey professionals has shifted national focus westward. In some respects, Alberta has begun to take a leading position on political and social issues within Canada. For example, Alberta's politicians have directly challenged the national government on issues such as health care and curtailment of greenhouse gases.

Diverse in Land and Culture

Alberta's growth since its establishment as a province in 1905 to a place of national power today has not been without turmoil. Some of the early conflicts between different groups of natives and settlers linger on to cause a deep-rooted divisiveness. While big cities like Edmonton and Calgary grow and many people thrive from the combination of low taxes and a churning economy, thousands of First Nations (native Indian tribes) and Métis peoples (French for "mixed," these have predominantly a dual native–white ancestry) feel left behind. They are battling to reclaim lands they felt were wrongfully taken while also reasserting the value of their culture and heritage, which they feel have been ignored and attacked over the last two hundred years.

Alberta's response to such challenges indicates a newfound concern for meeting the needs of all its people. Alberta led the way in establishing Métis land rights and settlements, and in beginning Métis child social services. The province is also actively negotiating land issues with First Nations peoples. First Nations societies have overcome years of social programs aimed at diminishing their heritage, and they have a renewed sense of their history and their connection to the land.

■ *Alberta's natural beauty includes a view of Lake Louise situated below the towering Canadian Rockies.*

■ *Alberta boasts residents as hearty and unique as the province's dynamic geography.*

Further, Alberta has opened itself to a wide range of people from different ethnic and religious backgrounds. During its settlement Alberta attracted diverse cultures, including Germans, Ukrainians, Chinese (many of whom stayed after helping to build the transcontinental railroad that crosses the province), and religious groups like the Mormons and Hutterians, who sought protection from prejudice in the United States. And despite racial tensions at the time of settlement, Alberta was a settlement area for many small, black populations who sought greater tolerance than they were finding in the United States.

Marked by a land that ranges from mountains to forests to prairies, Alberta is a diverse area with diverse people. In some way, Alberta's people have learned to survive, even thrive, in the face of difficult challenges posed by the land and by the people's own differences. The occasional western roughness of Alberta's people may hardly seem fitting for a princess, but the rough edge and the tough, surviving people continue to change the way Canada is shaped.

Prairies, Mountains, and Forests

Alberta's terrain ranges from the pancake-flat prairies of the southern section of the province to the massive and jagged Rocky Mountains in the west. Lesser known is the often densely forested regions surrounding dramatic river valleys in the north, as well as a belt of gently rolling aspen parklands across the center of the province. Alberta is hailed for its striking beauty because much of the land is still pristine wilderness nearly untouched by civilization. The varied terrain and northern climate have left parts of the province only sparsely populated, while the resources of the province as a whole contributed to the founding of two of Canada's biggest cities, Edmonton and Calgary. Each region, with its unique geography, plants, and animals, has long presented both opportunities and challenges for the people of Alberta.

The Many Faces of the Plains

Humans may have originally been attracted to the prairie region of southern Alberta by the abundant buffalo herds that roamed the area until the mid-nineteenth century. A hundred years ago, it was the possibilities for farming and ranching that drew people. The prairie area today is dotted with widely separated small towns and two small cities (Lethbridge and Medicine Hat), most of whose residents have come to appreciate the stark beauty of seemingly endless vistas of wheat fields and grasslands. In areas untouched by agriculture, the land seems not much changed from when the first Europeans began to explore this part of North

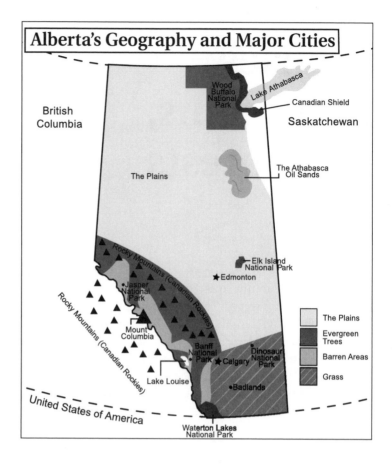

Alberta's Geography and Major Cities

America's prairies during the mid-nineteenth century. To them, the land appeared so untouched and unusable that visitors often commented on its "natural" character—its freedom from the realm of humanity.

The prairies can also seem bleak. In the late 1850s, Irishman John Palliser, one of the earliest surveyors of the prairie surrounding the area where present-day Alberta, Saskatchewan, and Montana meet, declared the land uninhabitable. This semiarid section of the prairies featured mostly low-lying grasses interspersed with occasional sage and cacti. Visitors to "Palliser's Triangle" today find some areas that are still barren and almost desert-like, as well as vast wheat fields where irrigation is possible. It is an area with few obvious distinctions between the United States and Canada. As historian Kenneth McNaught said, "The prairies are so integral a section of a north–south region that it is still possible along hundreds of miles of the Canadian–American border to be unsure of one's national location."[1]

But there is much more to the prairies than appears initially—the land has a character that shaped the people who lived on it. The prairie can also change dramatically from one locale to another. The land in Alberta to the north and northeast of Palliser's Triangle is considered mixed-grass prairie, characterized by a combination of shorter and taller grasses growing from two to four feet in height. The area enjoys more rain than does Palliser's Triangle and its dark brown soil is more fertile. Alberta's most productive farms and ranches are found in this mixed-grass prairie and the parklands belt bordering it to the north.

When It Rains on the Plains

The climate of Alberta's prairies, while more mild than that of the mountains or the forested north, can nevertheless try the patience of those who reside there. The area's location makes it conducive to weather extremes. Medicine Hat, for example, has been known to get as hot as 108° F (42° C) in the summer and as cold as –51° F (–46° C) in the winter. Fort Macleod in the southwest section of Alberta is where the province's hottest day occurred when the thermometer hit 110° F (43° C) on July 18, 1941.

Warm, dry chinook (from the name of a Pacific Northwest native tribe) winds can also bring unexpectedly warm weather even in the winter. Chinooks originate over the Pacific and lose their moisture as they rise over the western slopes of the Rockies. A chinook that swept into Lethbridge on January 15, 1971, raised the temperature from –4° F to 34° F (–20° C to 1° C) in one hour.

On the other hand, the plains can also experience extended periods of bone-chilling weather and devastating winter blizzards. Cold fronts that push down from the Arctic are sometimes accompanied by high winds that lead to dangerously cold conditions. In 1964 more than 1,000 livestock in the area of Red Deer were killed by a bitterly cold December storm. Three people also froze to death inside their homes when their heat went out during the night.

Throughout the year, sudden winds and thunderstorms can wreak havoc on the plains. Early Mormon settler Charles Card writes of traveling by buggy from one town to another when a sudden storm overtook him. "The wind and rain came on so strong," he notes, "I was obliged to turn the back of my wagon to the storm, put on the [brake] and unhitch & protect

■ Alberta's Dinosaur Badlands

In a few places the prairies in Alberta's southeastern corner are carved into barren badlands, water- and wind-cut canyons that form a nearly impassable terrain. Natives and early settlers alike declared such areas "bad for farming"—hence the name—because of the topography and lack of plant life. But Alberta's badlands are now recognized as a rich source of raw beauty and, in some cases, prehistoric findings.

Badlands in Alberta and other places in the west were carved by torrents of melting water that came from receding ice sheets more than twelve thousand years ago. The spillways appear to have been carved not by rivers but by flash floods. Erosion of the relatively soft sandstone has created many striking land features. Perhaps most notable are the hoodoos, soft-rock pillars topped with protective hard-rock caps. Many hoodoos have been eroded and carved into haunting shapes by the winds. In addition to the hoodoos, the area is marked by freestanding boulders, sinkholes that open into caverns, and deep gorges.

Alberta's most prominent badlands are found in Dinosaur Provincial Park, located about 125 miles (200 kilometers) east of Calgary. Geologist Joseph Burr Tyrrell discovered Alberta's first dinosaur fossil beds in nearby Drumheller in 1910. He found the skull of what is now called the Albertosaurus, a fierce, T. Rex-like flesh eater with sharp teeth, large claws, and strong hind legs. The finding set off a bone-collecting frenzy that has since led to the identification of some three dozen additional species of dinosaurs.

my horses by the wagon."[2] That storm passed within an hour, but many last longer and can cause flash flooding and crop damage. Alberta also experiences the occasional tornado.

Where Antelope Roam

Prairie weather demands that the plants and animals, like the people, must be rugged and adaptable. Trees are found mainly around water, or where farmers have planted windbreaks. More numerous are varieties of grasses that have adapted to survive weather extremes. Some have developed defenses against the brushfires that can spread rapidly, and destructively, through dry grass. As prairie writer Judy Schultz describes one grass,

> [Its] thick, ridged leaves resist evaporation, and its hollow stem and thick joints will bend in the wind without breaking. But here is the miraculous part, the special characteristic that allows it to survive: Because it grows from its base slightly below ground rather than from its tip, grass with-

Most of these findings have been within Dinosaur Provincial Park. The park is now recognized as one of the most important dinosaur fossil beds in the world and was designated a World Heritage Site by the United Nations Educational, Scientific and Cultural Organization (UNESCO) in 1979. Dinosaurs and other prehistoric animals thrived in the area because more than 65 million years ago it was a marshy, subtropical region, abundant with grasses and palms and bounded by a vast inland sea. (It is these ancient plants, decayed into carbonaceous fuels, that are responsible for the energy wealth existing beneath Alberta today.) Part of the park is open to tourists but whole sections are restricted and accessible only to scientists, who continue to excavate remains today.

■ *Hoodoos in Alberta's arid Badlands.*

stands almost any trauma, including fire, close cropping by hungry animals, even the repeated beating of hooves. And it seems to come back with renewed vigor.[3]

Settlement and farming has, however, radically changed Alberta's open plains over the past century. The native grass prairie as white settlers saw it exists in only a few pockets today. It was the vast expanses of these grasses that supported the plains bison, or buffalo, the most dominant animal of the prairie in the centuries prior to settlement. The power of their vast numbers was awe-inspiring. Bison that encountered trees could rub the bark off, leaving scars as high as six feet on the tree. Further, says the historian Gerald Friesen, "the bisons' roaring could be heard for miles and the path upon which the animals traveled resembled a war zone."[4] Bison have been making a comeback on the plains in recent years although not as wild herds. Rather, the vast majority of Alberta's 50,000 plains bison are being raised on some 800 ranches for the relatively healthy, low-fat meat.

■ *Alberta's vast plains region supports many animal species including buffalo.*

The prairie lands of Alberta also once held significant populations of prairie dogs and greater prairie chickens. Prairie dogs are short-tailed rodents of the squirrel family. The cross-continental explorers Meriwether Lewis and William Clark reported prairie dog populations that "could riddle the ground with burrows for several miles."[5] Some prairie dog underground colonies may have numbered in the millions. Prairie dog fossils can be found in southern Alberta but live populations no longer inhabit the province. Henlike greater prairie chickens, a type of grouse that thrived on the prairies after the decline of the buffalo, were wiped out by habitat loss as farms and ranches spread. Though extirpated (made locally extinct) from the province, populations of greater prairie chickens remain in prairie states such as Kansas.

The semiarid grasslands of southeast Alberta today provide prime habitat for pronghorn antelope, the fastest of all mammals and the last surviving species of a family of ungulates that once roamed widely in the North American prairies. Overhunting during the nineteenth century put pronghorns on the brink of extinction by 1900. In recent years the American and Canadian governments have protected pronghorns and in a few places successfully reintroduced them. Small numbers of lynx live in the north and west prairies, and bobcats hunt in the south.

The Parklands Belt

Where the prairies merge into the forests and uplands of the north, the land in Alberta changes into an unusual ecological zone known as parklands. The parklands belt does not extend all the way across Alberta. Rather, it is widest on the Saskatchewan border, roughly from Cold Lake to about the latitude of Red Deer. It extends into central Alberta past Edmonton and then narrows as it dips toward the foothills of the Rockies. The parklands belt ends somewhat north of Calgary, which is located on the border belt of the prairie and the foothills.

Alberta's parklands belt has rich soil and enough rainfall to support groves of aspen and poplar trees as well as sections of tall-grass prairie where the grass can run as high as five feet. Because this area is well suited to mixed farming, over time many of the trees have been cleared and about three-fourths of the land is cultivated. It is also the place where the province's population is most concentrated.

The parklands area has a somewhat moderate climate considering how far north it is. Although Edmonton is one of the most northerly large cities in the world, it is sunny, dry, and mild (daily highs during July and August average 70° F, or 21° C). In the winter months of January and February, Edmonton experiences daily highs that average 21° F (–6° C). This compares to daily highs during the same months that average 13° F (–11° C) in Winnipeg, Manitoba, which lies almost 250 miles (400 kilometers) south of Edmonton but is rarely reached by the warm chinook winds affecting Alberta.

The Majestic Rockies

The soaring Rocky Mountains stretch from Alberta's southeast corner, where the province intersects with British-Columbia to the west and Montana to the south, in a northwest direction up the Alberta/British Columbia border. Bordered by foothills to the east, the Canadian Rockies are craggy and rough-hewn, being geologically young enough not to have suffered the erosive effects that have smoothed over ranges like the Appalachians along North America's east coast. As dedicated mountaineers have noted, in the Alps of Europe "it is common to encounter polished and slippery knobs of rock on popular trails, whereas in the Rockies, the rock remains rough to both the touch and to boots. The soles of climbing boots wear quite quickly in the Rockies."[6]

Between 60 and 135 million years ago, the Canadian Rockies

■ *The Canadian Rockies, which include Mount Columbia, comprise Alberta's border with British Columbia.*

were formed when forces miles beneath the earth's crust thrust sedimentary rock upward, folding and piling it skyward. The lengthy chain of mountains that comprise the North American Rockies marks the continental divide, the line that determines whether rivers flow to the east, mostly to the Gulf of Mexico and thus eventually the Atlantic, or whether they flow to the west and empty into the Pacific. In a similar way, but unlike the American Rockies, the Canadian Rockies also divide the Arctic and Pacific Oceans. Most of Alberta's major river systems run from the Rockies, particularly from areas harboring some of the largest North American ice fields south of the Arctic. The Peace and Athabasca Rivers, which flow to the Arctic Ocean, and the Saskatchewan, which runs to Hudson Bay, all begin in the Rockies of Alberta. (The Milk River in southeastern Alberta is the only river in Canada to flow into larger rivers that eventually empty into the Gulf of Mexico.)

■ Climbing Mount Columbia

At 12,293 feet (3,747 meters), Mount Columbia is the highest peak in Alberta and the second highest in the Canadian Rockies (after Mount Robson in British Columbia). In 1898, explorers Herman Wooley and J. Norman Collie scaled nearby Mount Athabasca, which at the time was the highest ascent in the Rockies. From the summit, they saw Mount Columbia amid the huge Columbia Icefield. They attempted to scale the peak the next day but failed because of soft snow that masked numerous crevasses and drop-offs. The two tried and failed again in 1901, but did manage to map an important approach route through the Thompson Pass. Just as Wooley and Collie were about to attempt the climb again in 1902, another team of climbers announced they had reached the summit—thanks in part to Wooley's and Collie's map.

Mount Columbia is best known today as a classic Canadian ski ascent. The round-trip climb from the road to the summit and back usually takes three days; April and May are the months when conditions are best for attempted ascents. Most of the trip is on skis, although the uppermost peak is an almost forty-degree snow slope that requires hiking boots fitted with crampons (metal spikes). Fast-moving storms that can envelop the mountain in snow or fog for days at a time present a frequent danger. The many deep crevasses on the glacial approach to Columbia are a hazard even during good conditions. Parties of skiers typically rope together to prevent the lead skier from plunging to his or her death in a crevasse hidden by a thin layer of surface snow. Climbers also often use four-foot bamboo stakes topped with black flags to mark out the safe course between crevasses.

Like the plains, the mountains experience extremes of weather. Moisture-laden clouds borne by prevailing winds out of the west dump up to 100 feet (30 meters) of snow on western sections of the Canadian Rockies during the winter. (More of this snow falls in British Columbia than Alberta, since the continental divide marks the border between the two provinces up to where the divide hits the 120° line of latitude. The mountain slopes and foothills on the eastern, Alberta side of the Rockies are thus somewhat warmer and drier.) Many peaks, like Mount Columbia, see frequent whiteout conditions from wind-driven snow. Glaciers survive year-round in the Columbia Icefield and elsewhere in the Rockies. The Columbia Icefield is a remnant of the last huge ice sheet to recede from northern Canada. The Columbia Icefield is now an important tourist attraction along the national park area from Banff in the south to Jasper.

Plants and Animals of the Rockies

The forbidding glaciers, tall summits, and alpine meadows of Alberta's Rockies harbor a surprising range of plant and animal life. Depending upon altitude, the central zone of the Rockies is hospitable to wildflowers, shrubs, and coniferous trees that extend up from the foothills. The larch trees that grow at high elevations in the central mountains have needles that turn a distinctive shade of yellow before dropping to the ground each September. The cold temperatures of the northern areas lead to a somewhat more restricted array of species, with lichens and stunted trees at high altitudes. Many mountain valleys are covered in grass. Lower average rainfall levels in the southern mountains mean that the plant life there is also comparatively less lush.

Where the plains from the east encounter the Rockies in southern Alberta, there are fewer of the foothills that border the central and northern mountain regions. Thus the southern mountains seem even more dramatic, rising without warning to lofty and jagged peaks. The mountains here support eagles, hawks, and other large raptors as well as varieties of wolves, mountain goats, and sheep. Black bears, common throughout much of North America and Canada, are striking here because they vary in color from cinnamon to deep black. In the area's Waterton Lakes National Park, alpine meadows merge into grasslands rather than forests and attract crowd-pleasing populations of elk and deer.

■ The Rockies' Banff and Jasper National Parks

Beyond their influence on river flow and weather patterns, Alberta's mountains offer breathtaking views and spectacular hikes that attract visitors from all over the world. Two of Canada's most popular national parks, Banff and Jasper, begin a mere 70 miles (110 kilometers) west of Calgary. Banff National Park, set aside in 1885, is Canada's oldest national park. Founded in 1907, Jasper National Park is contiguous to Banff to its north. The area covered by these parks is remarkably diverse, marked by mountains, glaciers, ice fields, lakes, and canyons. Lying east of the continental divide, this region also has more meadows and alpine areas than land west of the divide. Large mammals including deer, bighorn sheep, black and grizzly bears, and elk make their home here.

While much of the terrain in Banff and Jasper is good for hiking and skiing, it grows particularly harsh in the winter. Midway through the winter, the backcountry can be accessed only by skis. By January, temperatures may drop as low as –22° F (–30° C) for a week at a time.

Running from Lake Louise to Jasper and just west of Banff is the spectacular Icefields Parkway, a 143-mile (230-kilometer) drive through wilderness only occasionally marked by a gas station, lodge, or campground. The drive passes through forests and canyons; glaciers can be reached by a short hike in spots. It is possible to make the drive in a few hours, "But it's likely," Andrew Hempstead notes in *Alberta and the Northwest Territories Handbook*, "you'll want to spend at least a day, probably more, stopping at each of the 13 viewpoints, hiking the trails, watching the abundant wildlife, and just generally enjoying one of the world's most magnificent landscapes."

In all, it is impossible to live in Alberta without being touched by the influence of the Rockies. The mountains are unique and in some spots almost unexplored treasures. They provide a home to ancient remnants of continental glaciers, breathtaking canyons and meadows, and plants and animals found in few other places in Alberta. Unlike the far north of the province, though, the mountain areas are somewhat more accessible and hospitable to the residents and visitors alike.

The Northern Forest

Geography and climate determine the features of much of the northern half of Alberta. Just north of Edmonton, the parkland stands of aspens and poplars merge into coniferous forests featuring pine, fir, and spruce trees. Farther north, the landscape is more austere. Above the permafrost line that runs across Alberta south of the Peace River and north of Fort McMurray, forests give way to marshy highlands and areas of exposed rock where the glacier-scoured landscape offers limited opportunities for plant life. The year-round frozen soil (at varying depths) of permafrost prevents large, deep-rooted trees from taking hold. Only the occasional stunted conifer and sprawling moss and lichens thus mark many areas. In western Alberta, south of the permafrost line, lies a surprisingly verdant area. This is the section of the Peace River valley that extends from the town of Peace River to the British Columbia border. It supports logging and even the northernmost wheat fields in North America.

In general, the harsh winter temperatures of the far north discourage many forms of plant and animal life, including humans, as historian Andrew Malcolm notes in his description of the tiny communities and the raw characters they attract:

> Some of these communities are former frontier forts, where furs changed hands for knives. Some are disposable towns, there to mine the ground while the price is right in Germany or Japan, and then to disappear. Others are mere outposts, just camps, where residents get extra isolation pay and wily wolves eat unwary pets. There, frozen rivers become local roadways. Airplanes are the only reliable link to the "outside." And trackless trains of bulldozers dragging huge skidding sleds of fuel and food to distant settlements crunch their way through long winters and woods and frozen swamps at four or five miles an hour.[7]

The most northeastern corner of Alberta, north of Lake Athabasca, is an extension of the underlying Canadian Shield. This is a vast and ancient structural unit of the earth's crust. It is vaguely horseshoe-shaped around Hudson Bay and covers much of eastern and central Canada. Geologically, the shield is made up of Precambrian rocks that date to more than 600 million years ago. In effect, the shield is the underlying foundation of the continental north, and much of it surfaces in granite and other rock. In many places the soil was easily scraped off this exposed rock by the numerous glaciers that advanced and retreated over North America within the past 2 million years.

Although conditions are harsh in Alberta's northern forests, the area also offers pristine wilderness, plant and animal life largely untouched by the progress of humanity, and a

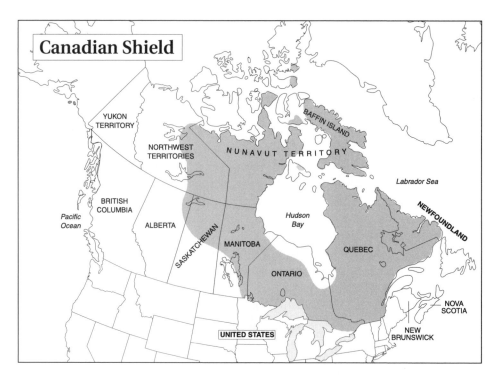

Canadian Shield

wealth of often-overlooked beauty. Ray Rasmussen, a devoted admirer of Alberta's north, says the areas are "little-known, little-visited, and only vaguely imagined by Albertans"[8] in large part because there are so few visitors.

Land of Highland Lakes

Located along the Alberta/Saskatchewan border and just south of Lake Athabasca, the Athabasca Plain is home to some of Alberta's most striking and untouched scenery. The area around Lake Athabasca, which is partly in Saskatchewan, is particularly spectacular. "The locals refer to this sweep of shoreline as Alberta's best-kept secret—and for good reason," says Rasmussen. "Granite headlands and bright sand beaches stretch from Fidler Point to White Sand Point and beyond. The landscape has never been scarred by industrial activity and the feel of trackless wilderness is nearly absolute."[9] Summer temperatures average in the mid-50° F (low teens C) and some 12 inches (300 millimeters) of rain per year support a fair range of wildlife.

The lake area differs significantly from the shield area of northeastern Alberta, with its scrub plants, mosses, and lichen. Around Lake Athabasca, many highly adaptable species of plants and trees persist. The area is home to tansy, bladder-wort, rush, and starwort. Dominant trees include the white spruce, jack pine, and black spruce, and thus far, most of these

■ Where the Buffalo Roam

Much less visited than popular Banff and Jasper, Alberta's Wood Buffalo National Park is an overlooked natural asset. It was established in 1922 and bridges north-central Alberta and the Northwest Territories. Wood Buffalo is huge. More than twice the size of Massachusetts, it is the second-largest national park in the world (after one in Greenland). Wood Buffalo is also remote. To reach its one entry road by auto, you have to drive more than 800 miles (1,300 kilometers) north from Edmonton to the town of Hay River, on the southern shores of the Great Slave Lake in the Northwest Territories, and from there to park headquarters in Fort Smith (with much of this last leg consisting of a gravel road with no services).

Once there you can see a wide range of unusual habitats, including one of the largest freshwater deltas in the world, shallow lakes, forested uplands, and streams that meander through bogs and meadows. You can also see a large free-ranging herd of mixed plains and wood buffalo. The wood buffalo is a taller, heavier, and darker subspecies of the plains buffalo. A century ago as many as 170,000 wood buffalo ranged in areas north of the plains buffalo, especially in northern Alberta and nearby parts of British Columbia and the Northwest Territories. Wood Buffalo National Park's herd of 2,000 hybrid buffalo actually resulted from some questionable wildlife management by government officials in the 1920s. Because plains buffalo were starting to become too numerous in a park near Wainwright, Alberta, officials moved some to Wood Buffalo, which had only a small wood buffalo herd. Unfortunately, the plains buffalo carried cattle-derived bovine tuberculosis and brucellosis. The plains/wood buffalo descendants at Wood Buffalo now carry these diseases, and any that stray can pose a threat to the 3,000 or so disease-free wood buffalo alive, mostly in recovery herds in parks in the Northwest Territories. Wood Buffalo's mixed-bison herd thus faces an uncertain future. Some officials have even advocated slaughtering the entire herd, so that true wood buffalo can again roam the park, an area that once represented almost half of its natural range.

Wood Buffalo National Park is also the summer breeding ground for the world's largest flock of whooping cranes. Wildlife officials estimate that only 320 of these majestic birds exist worldwide today, up from as few as 14 in the early 1940s. From April to September, a flock estimated at 170 whoopers nests in marshes in the northern reaches of the park, taking off each fall for the 2,500-mile (4,000-kilometer) flight to their winter grounds in Aransas National Wildlife Refuge in Texas.

■ *A ceremonial assembly of Blood Indians gathers on once native-owned land, now property of the Banff Hotel seen in the background.*

have been untouched by logging or heavy industry. Intermingled with the trees are groundplants like bearberry as well as American dune grass, fungi, and reindeer lichens.

Because so much of the Athabasca Plain remains unexplored in detail, little is known of the region's unique animals, but some important, well-documented species either make their homes here or come to breed or hunt. Arctic and Caspian terns, both subarctic species, have occasionally wandered south, and sandhill cranes have been known to breed here. In the rugged upland areas west of the Athabasca Plain, cooler temperatures and poorer soil make for even tougher conditions for wildlife. The many river systems do help support beaver and moose. Barren ground caribou, the rare willow ptarmigan, and arctic fox have also been known to wander down from farther north and breed in the area. Bald eagle and osprey are also common to the region, particularly around the lakes. Golden eagles often nest on the cliffs, and the protected peregrine falcon has also been spotted.

The northern region remains a remote and somewhat mysterious area of Alberta. Aside from early trappers and native peoples who hunted in the region, and with the exception of a handful of modern dwellers and travelers, people have largely ignored this part of Alberta. Its remoteness allows it to serve as a last-chance haven for species like the whooping crane, although even here the land is not immune from potential development and use for logging, hydroelectric power, or mining.

Land Is Destiny

Alberta's land can be severe and unforgiving. It may seem that people who live there must battle the elements—the droughts, the thunderstorms, the brushfires, the fierce cold—just to carve out an existence. Such difficulty has always bred strong-willed people. While working and struggling with the land, the people have also clashed in their relations with each other.

The Fur Trade and the First Nations

W hen Europeans first encountered Alberta's native peoples, they found diverse societies steeped in ancient traditions, skilled in using the land's resources for survival, and adept at intertribal trade. But each group had a different culture and lifestyle, and as a result often-conflicting goals. While First Nations peoples worked with settlers, opening trade routes and hunting furs, they also were devastated by the settlers' hunger for land and by the diseases they carried. Early relations among native peoples, settlers, and the Métis were often tense, and rebellions and fighting broke out. Treaties ended many of the clashes at the time, but the tensions still exist and much of Alberta's early history seems to linger among the people today in their diversity, their conflicts, their struggles with the land, and their battles for social equality.

The Blackfoot Nation

The tribes that early European traders found in Alberta had carved complex, diverse societies out of the land. In the mid-1700s, numerous tribes roamed different regions of Alberta, including most notably Blackfoot tribes in the central and south, Cree tribes in the east and across the parklands, and the Beaver, Chipewyan, and Slavey tribes in the north and west. Each adapted its society to the resources available from the land and the relationships they had with other tribes, ranging from friendly trade to occasional warfare.

The Blackfoot were perhaps the most numerous of Alberta's First Nations peoples. Their carefully structured society helped them dominate, at the height of their power before the coming of Europeans, territory from the Rocky Mountains to the present-day Saskatchewan border and from the Missouri River to the North Saskatchewan River. Three main tribes made up the Blackfoot nation: the Blackfoot proper (also known as the Siksika), the Blood, and the Peigan. They shared a common linguistic background, speaking tongues of the Algonquian-Wakashan language.

Blackfoot tribes typically lived as families in bands. Such bands could be as small as ten lodges or as large as thirty lodges and typically included 80 to 240 persons. Each band was led by a respected leader, and the rest of the band might be composed of the leader's family as well as others who might not be related. The bands were carefully organized to minimize conflict and strengthen unity among the people. Band members were free to leave at any time and join other bands. This structure meant that many people avoided difficulty simply by leaving conflicts behind for other bands. Such flexible cohesiveness also allowed for greater hunting and social success.

The leader of the band was at once a central, powerful figure, but also one chosen by his peers for his qualities. Thus, he could not coerce his followers but could only lead those who were willing to be led. As one authority has noted, while the leader had to be a good warrior, "most importantly, he had to be generous. The Blackfoot despised a miser!"[10] So central was the leader that his death might break up the band.

The Blackfoot relied on both individual and communal buffalo hunts to sustain them throughout the year. According to the Provincial Museum of Alberta, which has documented early native life in the province, individual hunting of plains buffalo and other game was common—"in summer, a wolf skin might be worn as a disguise since the buffalo would allow wolves to approach closely; in winter, a white blanket hid the hunter as he stalked the herd."[11] But the summer communal hunts, including the driving of herds off of "buffalo jumps," were the most important of the year.

The Blackfoot not only managed well their own survival, they organized so effectively that they were particularly successful at fighting off intruders, both native and white. Other tribes such as the Plains Cree adapted somewhat differently to the coming of whites.

The Plains Cree

The Cree who eventually lived in the northern plains and the parklands belt of Alberta originated as an Algonquian-speaking

■ Head-Smashed-In Buffalo Jump

Not far from both the British Columbia and Montana borders in southwestern Alberta, Head-Smashed-In Buffalo Jump is one of the few preserved buffalo jumps. Driving herds of plains buffalo off of a cliff is a Native North American communal hunting technique that ensured the survival of the band by harvesting many buffalo at a time. Native peoples started to use the Head-Smashed-In jump more than fifty-five hundred years ago and continued to use it until the late 1800s, when the buffalo were driven into near extinction.

Band members would use natural land features and specially constructed drivelines, to direct buffalo to the jump. Hunters built the drivelines with piles of rocks that they arranged like a funnel. Some hunters would drive the herd toward the drivelines. Other hunters would leap out from behind the rock piles and wave robes to frighten the buffalo and keep them inside the lines. Ultimately, the buffalo would run over the cliff to their deaths, and native peoples could harvest the meat, skins, and other materials.

Visitors to Head-Smashed-In (the name comes from a Blackfoot legend about the fate of a hunter who stood too close to the cliff bottom as a particularly large herd barreled over the top) Buffalo Jump can view the sandstone cliff jump and visit a new interpretive center, which has exhibits relating to Blackfoot ecology, mythology, lifestyle, and technology.

■ *Head-Smashed-In Buffalo Jump, in southwestern Alberta, features a wide expanse of sheer cliffs.*

woodland people in eastern Canada. They traveled by canoe, or snowshoe and toboggan, and relied primarily on moose, caribou, ducks, and geese for food. The Woodland Cree were adept traders who partnered with early European fur traders to move goods across the continent. While the first European contact with Alberta native peoples did not happen until 1754, when trader Anthony Henday of the Hudson's Bay Company first made the trek from eastern Canada into Alberta to find more tribes to trade with, European goods were by then already well rooted within the tribes. Cree middlemen and traders had effectively forged markets among the Alberta native peoples and had transported European goods for years.

By the mid-eighteenth century bands of Cree had begun to settle permanently on the plains, which were already occupied by other native tribes. Much of the Cree's woodland knowledge and activity needed to be replaced—the horse took over for the canoe as transport, buffalo for caribou as food. The highly structured and aggressive Plains Cree also eagerly adopted a number of European innovations, especially the use of guns in hunting and fighting.

Like the Blackfoot, during most of the year the Plains Cree lived in nomadic bands that hunted buffalo. During the summers, the plentiful buffalo food allowed them to gather in large encampments for ceremonies and socializing. They based their religion on relationships with animals and spirits that revealed themselves in dreams. And like the Blackfoot, they had strong leaders whose traits were recognized not because of might or power but because of careful relations with others. Writer Richard J. Preston says,

> People tried to show respect for each other by an ideal ethic of noninterference, in which each individual was responsible for his or her actions and the consequences of his or her actions. Leaders in group hunts, raids and trading were granted authority in directing such tasks, but otherwise the ideal was to lead by means of exemplary action and discreet suggestion.[12]

The Beaver, Slavey, and Chipewyan Tribes

Less powerful than the Blackfoot and Cree nations were a trio of tribes that came to occupy the northern portions of present-day Alberta. At one time, the Beaver lived in a large territory that stretched from the Peace River into central Alberta and Saskatchewan. But like their cousins the Slavey and Chipewyan, the Beaver lacked the tight organization of the Blackfoot and

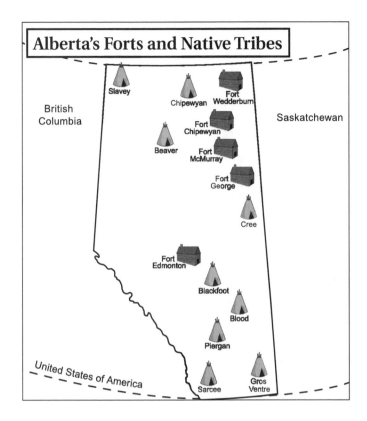

Alberta's Forts and Native Tribes

Slavey

Chipewyan Fort Wedderburn

British Columbia

Saskatchewan

Fort Chipewyan

Beaver Fort McMurray

Fort George

Cree

Fort Edmonton

Blackfoot

Blood

Piergan

United States of America

Sarcee Gros Ventre

the firearms and horses of the Cree and were eventually driven north and west.

All three tribes were generally peaceful and well adapted to the river-and-lake environment of the northern woodland areas. The Slavey lived primarily on fish, small game, and some moose and caribou; they often struggled to obtain food. The Beaver, known as exceptional hunters, and the Chipewyan generally relied more on big game, particularly moose.

The three tribes differed somewhat in their strengths, levels of organization, and traditions. The Chipewyan generally treasured flexibility and personal freedom. They did not organize for warfare, although like the Beaver they considered the Plains Cree their enemies. The Slavey usually kept to the forests in small family groups, and thus they had few enemies. Like their cousins, they rarely organized, but conflict caused them to choose leaders on occasion. They were generally known for a rich heritage of storytelling. Though driven west by the Plains Cree, the Beaver were generally considered strong warriors. Like their cousins, they spoke an Athapaskan-rooted language that originated in the upper central and western portions of what is now Canada.

Trading Companies Vie for Territory

Anthony Henday was the first European known to visit the territory of present-day Alberta. His 1754 visit did not bring immediate results for his employer, the Hudson's Bay Company, and he found that European goods were already traded regularly among native peoples. Even so, his visit was a signal of the rivalries and settlements to come.

Henday was only the first of many emissaries to come from the Hudson's Bay Company, the powerful British fur trading enterprise that had spread from the east coast of Canada and was looking for new markets and new suppliers. In the 1780s

■ The Travels of Anthony Henday

When British-born Anthony Henday set out from York Factory, a trading post established on the Hudson Bay (in present-day Manitoba) in 1684 by the Hudson's Bay Company, down the Hayes River in June 1754, he probably did not imagine that his journey would take him farther into North America's west than any previous white man. By the time he and the party of Plains Cree who accompanied him as guides returned almost a year later, his more than 2,000-mile (3,200-kilometer) round-trip journey had taken him into present-day Alberta as far as the foothills of the Rockies.

By the fall of 1754, after traveling down rivers and over land past a number of rival French forts, Henday reached the plains of present-day western Saskatchewan. Though historians still debate his exact route, Henday is thought to have entered the area of present-day Alberta along the Battle River valley, south of present-day Lloydminster. In October Henday's party came upon a great Blackfoot camp, apparently somewhere south of where Red Deer is today. Henday was greeted with hospitality and deference, feasting and smoking the calumet (a long ceremonial pipe) with the chief and elders. Henday attempted to interest the natives in returning with him to the Hudson Bay, and more generally in working as traders for his company. But in the end, the chiefs said that the buffalo supplied most of their needs, European goods were routinely traded in the area, and they felt no need to endanger their people on journeys to barter for goods they already received.

Henday reached the Rockies in late December before determining he could go no farther. He and his party remained in the region of the North Saskatchewan River until the spring of 1755, hunting buffalo for survival, before at last beginning their return journey. When he and his men made it back to York Factory in June with canoes bearing furs and other trade goods, he was greeted with a barrage of celebratory gunfire.

■ Fort Edmonton Park

Visitors to Fort Edmonton Park in Edmonton can take a step back into the fur trading days. The largest historical park in Canada, the park is a faithful reconstruction of the fur trading post as it was in the mid-1840s. Within the fort's log palisades and bastions are more than a dozen buildings, including a blacksmith shop, chapel, boatshed, and trade store.

The fort's technology is particularly interesting. Hoping to reduce their reliance on outside food sources, the men built a windmill and planted fields around the fort with wheat, barley, and oats to be milled. Today, Fort Edmonton Park includes a 51-foot-tall replica of the windmill. Another interesting feature is the ice house, which stored meat. The ice house was built over a pit, and it was enclosed by two walls separated by a foot of earth for insulation. A sod roof also helped keep the interior cool.

■ *A walk down the main street of Fort Edmonton is like stepping back in time.*

the Montreal-based North West Company emerged as a successful rival. Over the next forty years, the two trading companies, as well as the French, competed fiercely for cooperation and trade with various First Nations. Officers of the trading companies, including Henday and Scottish-born Alexander Mackenzie of the North West Company, were among the first Europeans to explore Canada, though always with an eye on expanding the fur trade. The "North Westers," as they were called, were particularly active explorers and in general were more willing than the Hudson's Bay traders to leave their forts and work among natives. "The North Westers looked upon their competitors with more contempt than hostility," notes historian George Woodcock, "and in a way their contempt was justified, for the [Hudson's Bay] Company was unfit to wage a war of trade. The loose partnership of the North Westers allowed great scope for independent initiative."[13]

In 1788, the North West Company built Fort Chipewyan on the southwest shore of Lake Athabasca in present-day Alberta. This location was ideal for exploration and fur trade because of its proximity to an extensive network of rivers, including the Peace, Athabasca, and Slave. The fort quickly became a lively "Emporium of the North" supporting a mix of European and First Nations peoples. In a pattern typical of the companies' bitter competition, the Hudson's Bay Company responded by building Fort Wedderburn in the same area.

Over the next decade the two companies established more than a dozen forts on rivers throughout present-day Alberta. While many forts lasted only a few years, forts like the two built in 1795 on the North Saskatchewan River at the site of present-day Edmonton later became the foundations for major cities in Alberta and elsewhere. Fort Chipewyan is now the oldest continuously occupied settlement in the province. The trading companies' often-strained relations with First Nations peoples also set the stage for some of Alberta's present-day social problems.

Life on the Frontier

Everyday life for traders and others in the first western forts was challenging. Even though the rivals from the Hudson's Bay and North West Companies were mostly cordial with each other, their competition made conditions increasingly difficult in the years before the companies' merger in 1821. The forts' clerks, who recorded the trades and did the accounting, seem to have lived better than the traders. Those inside an early–nineteenth-century frontier fort might at least have had access to such luxuries as chamber pots, clothes with buckles and ornaments, and combs. Traders, on the other hand, typically wore rough clothing, had to go off hunting during the day, and enjoyed few luxuries. In some cases, residents of nearby rival forts might have traded necessities. Competition could also be cutthroat—at least one fort let a rival face starvation during a particularly harsh winter.

Regardless of the competition, the presence of the Europeans continued to alter the way of life of First Nations peoples. When partnerships between Europeans and First Nations grew stronger, many natives settled around the company forts as a means of speeding up trade and bettering their livelihood. Many of the first forts were slowly transformed from fortified enclosures to small towns, with First Nations and white families settling outside the walls and growing crops. The mixing of native peoples and Europeans also resulted in interracial marriages and relationships, especially between French fur traders and native women. These eventually gave rise to a new people, the Métis.

The Hardy Prairie Métis

The term *Métis* originally referred to children who had a French parent and a native parent. Some writers have used the term to include all children born to a native parent and a European parent. Today, it generally refers to descendants of French and native ancestors or descendants of Scottish or English and native ancestors, usually from the era of fur trading in the 1700s and 1800s.

The Métis of the plains grew accustomed to the harsh conditions, mixing readily among native peoples and Europeans while struggling to maintain their livelihoods. Many Métis spoke native languages; if their first language was European-based, they laced their speech with native words and expressions. Historians often credit the prairie Métis with an unusual hardiness that exceeded that of the eastern Métis.

■ The Mixed Identity of the Métis

The mixed identity of the Métis people is reflected in their history. They were at once bound to native traditions and trained in the skills of horsemanship, shooting, and commercial hunting. But the Métis were also raised to have knowledge of European culture and society. Many chose the semi-nomadic existence of prairie natives, while others settled on farms or worked in the trading posts.

The Métis' mixed heritage led to many difficulties for the people, caught as they were between two very different cultures. An inherent tension often existed between husband and wife. For example, the Provincial Museum of Alberta, commenting on the human history of the fur trade, speculates on the Indian/Scottish marriage of Sitting Still and Charles McTavish, a couple who lived in one of the old forts: "[Sitting Still was] missing less and less the nomadic ways of her own people. Her two children gave her great joy, but the oldest one frightened her a little. He was so smart, too smart. She knew that her husband was thinking of sending the boy away to school, and if he went she feared she would lose him completely to the white men's ways."

This tension seems to have played out across the people as a whole. Many Métis never learned to read or write and were raised in relative poverty. Their homes were typically made of spruce or pine logs with gaps filled in by clay; thatch or bark was used to cover the roofs. Parchment took the place of windows. Only a minority of Métis were raised in a European, middle-class lifestyle, and they considered themselves closer to white than native. Those who could obtain an education often learned agriculture, trading, or business skills that helped them manage better in the shifting economy.

■ *A group of nomadic Métis traders in their prairie camp.*

"Their essentially nomadic existence accustomed the western Métis to a hard climate and perhaps gave them greater endurance than the Métis of Assiniboia [in central Canada],"[14] notes Métis scholar Marcel Giraud. Other commentators have agreed and noted that the Métis had a physical vigor that approached or even surpassed that of some native peoples.

The Métis nevertheless faced the problem of being recognized as a distinct society. Though they partnered freely with Europeans in commercial hunting (often to the resentment of native peoples), the Métis were later left out of the treaty process that affected many First Nations in the second half of the nineteenth century. The deals the Métis eventually struck with provincial governments were generally even less favorable than the one-sided treaties signed by the First Nations peoples.

Although the methods of hunting, the social organizations, and the traditions of the Métis and the many First Nations differed, these societies faced similar challenges. Ultimately all were profoundly changed by the rise and fall of the fur trade and the advent of farming and ranching. Even today, some of the strained relations between the diverse groups of people who came together in Alberta can be traced back to much earlier times.

Beaver to Buffalo

As the fur trade developed during the early nineteenth century, it changed the ways native peoples and Europeans related to each other. In earlier times, the trade relied mostly on the fur of beavers and other small animals. In the years following the merger of the Hudson's Bay and North West Companies, however, the European market shifted. Beaver became increasingly scarce and more and more buyers wanted the meat or hides of buffalo.

The plains buffalo had largely been a source of food, shelter (hides were used to make tepees), and clothing for the native peoples, but the shift in the market now made it an important trading commodity. The Métis, in particular, were instrumental in helping European traders hunt and kill vast numbers of buffalo. It is estimated that the Hudson's Bay Company bought more than half a million buffalo hides in the 1860s and 1870s. The Métis were also major suppliers of pemmican, the dried buffalo meat powder that became a frontier staple because it was easily stored and shipped.

Buffalo were not the only animals slaughtered with abandon. Judy Schultz, a descendant of prairie settlers, writes:

> Large wolf packs that had followed the migrating buffalo met the same fate, and many thousands of wolves were poisoned by itinerant hunters known as wolfers, so named because it was their practice to lace a dead animal (frequently a buffalo carcass) with strychnine and swing back later to skin out the poisoned wolves and collect the hides.[15]

By the mid-1880s the plains buffalo herds, which had contained as many as 30 to 70 million animals two centuries earlier, and the wolf packs that had provided so much for the native peoples were virtually extinct.

With the decline of the plains buffalo, the First Nations' nomadic way of life was also disappearing. In the mid-1800s, trading centers like those at Fort Edmonton, Fort Chipewyan, and Upper Fort Gary (which eventually became Winnipeg, Manitoba) attracted fair numbers of Métis and native peoples who desired to make trade more efficient. Many mixed with the Europeans, producing more Métis people and altering their nomadic habits. In addition, as the years passed, more traders and others settled near the forts and began to claim the land. Many tribes had little notion of land ownership because they migrated with the seasons and used the land not as a permanent living station but as a means of survival. Consequently, European settlers often easily snatched up native lands and offered little or no compensation to the tribes who had used it for centuries.

Missionaries Make Inroads

In concert with these changes, in the mid-nineteenth century European missionaries began to filter into the area. In 1818, the Roman Catholic Church sent a pair of priests to the Red River valley in present-day Manitoba, and an Anglican clergyman followed in 1820. Initially, these religious men preached primarily to the traders and their families, but ministries were soon extended to the First Nations peoples. The spread of European religion followed in the footsteps of the European traders, and the Methodist Robert Rundle eventually started a mission at Fort Edmonton in 1840 and inspired the building of another at Pigeon Lake, south of Fort Edmonton, in 1848. Catholic and Anglican missionaries had also arrived in the area by 1875.

European observers tended to misunderstand the rituals and symbols of native peoples, and thus believed that much of their religion was mere superstition. In many cases missionaries successfully converted natives and Métis. These efforts eventually had such a deep impact on native and Métis lives that it was common for missionaries to accompany Métis hunters on the buffalo hunt and to minister at native wintering grounds. Today, many First Nations peoples in particular are striving to revive lost spiritual traditions.

Toward a Confederation

The rapid changes the area was experiencing came to a climax in the late 1860s. In 1867, the British Parliament passed the British North America Act, in effect allowing its Canadian colonies to opt for inclusion in a Canadian confederation. The "Dominion of Canada" would still be a British colony but would be self-governed and have other powers of nationhood. Four colonies (Ontario, Quebec, Nova Scotia, and New Brunswick) voted for confederation (Prince Edward Island and Newfoundland rejected confederation at the time) and on July 1, 1867, the modern country of Canada was born.

The new government was immediately faced with the problem of the status of the huge tracts of land to the north and west of Ontario. Much of this was still "Rupert's Land," the area granted the Hudson's Bay Company in its 1670 charter from the king of England. The new Canadian government began negotiating with the Hudson's Bay Company to purchase this land and in 1870 managed to buy it. The Canadian government then had a freer hand to expand settlement on the prairies and encourage agriculture in this area, which it named the Northwest Territories. Government officials also planned the country's first intercontinental railroad.

First Nations in Decline

Europeans had brought firearms and horses to the native peoples and thus had strengthened the power of some tribes, but ultimately the spread of white society was disastrous for the First Nations. Perhaps the greatest harm Europeans caused was inadvertent—they carried infectious diseases, like smallpox, that were new to native peoples. Lacking the degree of resistance that the Europeans had built up to these diseases over centuries, native societies experienced appalling mortality rates of up to 90 percent. And while Europeans had learned about the benefits of quarantining the ill, the native custom of bringing family members and healers to the bedsides of the dying likely contributed to spreading the diseases.

Frontier trade practices were often financially unfair and socially damaging, particularly as they introduced alcohol to native peoples. The liquor-for-fur trade became so profitable that American traders established a number of "whiskey posts" with names like Fort Whoop-Up in the 1860s in present-day southern Alberta. The alcohol, eventually called firewater among plains people, varied in its strength and potency since it was prepared homemade by traders and sellers. An 1899 recipe, now kept at the Glenbow Institute in Calgary, seems typical and shows some of the powerful ingredients that helped damage native health and eventually tore apart tribal family relationships:

> Fort Whoop-Up Recipe for the liquor traded to Indians:
>
> Rx alcohol (S.P.R.) 1 qt.
> Black strap chewing tobacco—1 lb.
> Jamaica ginger—1 bottle
> Black molasses—1 quart
> Water—q.s.
> The whole boiled until "ripe"
> A cup of the above for one buffalo hide[16]

The new Canadian government became increasingly concerned about the whiskey trade, the forts, and the general lawlessness developing in the area. In 1874 it sent three hundred Northwest Mounted Police to restore order. The worst of the whiskey trade ended, but what was left of the First Nations peoples would soon find themselves unable to resist the oncoming tide of European settlers.

Treaties and Scrips

Soon after confederation the Canadian government began negotiating treaties with the First Nations peoples. Having been
devastated by disease, alcohol, and the loss of the buffalo,
tribes were in a weakened position. Eventually, most Alberta-
area tribes signed either Treaty 6, 7, or 8, thus surrendering all
aboriginal rights to prairie land to the government. In return,
they were to receive reservation land, cash, education, and
other incentives.

While this transition was generally more peaceful than the
transition to reservation life among the Native Americans in
the United States, it fostered deep problems and discontent.
Native peoples who had viewed land not as something to be
owned but something to be used for survival found themselves
forced into agriculture, often on marginal and infertile land. In
addition, their nomadic lifestyles had not prepared them for
such a shift to farming. Further, over the years many have felt
that the government has not kept all of its promises in the
agreements. Today, court battles continue over land rights and
over further incentives to be provided First Nations peoples,
many of whom suffer from poverty and poor education.

In part because of their mixed identity, the Métis were ignored in the treaty process. Stripped of their land rights and no
longer free to roam the plains, they suffered even more debilitating poverty. In the late 1800s, the Canadian government
tried to address the problems by issuing scrip certificates, which
would allow the Métis to purchase land. Later, the government
allowed scrips to be exchanged for either land or cash. However,
in part because the Métis saw land in much the same way native peoples did, many sold their scrips to land speculators at
fractions of the land's value. Today, court cases persist that try
to rectify land disputes dating back to the issuance of scrips.

In reality, the transitional period had only begun for native peoples. After the 1880s, when the transcontinental railroad linked Alberta to coastal ports, waves of ranchers and
farmers would arrive with new ideas about commerce and
new products to trade. The centuries of wandering fur traders
and nomadic bands of buffalo hunters were over, and the century of settlement was about to begin.

Settling the West

T he treaties the Canadian government signed with the First Nations peoples effectively cleared the open lands for farming, ranching, and city development. The government wasted little time in orchestrating a massive migration that would run from the 1890s to the First World War. During this time, thousands of immigrants came from Europe and America to the loosely policed, wide-open prairies for cheap farmland or ranch land. Towns sprang up, boomed, and receded with the rise and fall of the local economy. Fortunes were made and lost in ranching and land speculation. In a sense, the development of this unbridled cowboy era of the Canadian west set the stage for the oil barons and Internet entrepreneurs who now come to Alberta for its entrepreneurial free spirit.

But the time period was also one of struggle for First Nations and Métis peoples, as well as newcomers including Mormons, Hutterians (a Christian religious sect), and blacks from America. The First Nations peoples in particular, newly established on reservation lands, often suffered devastating poverty while the economy roared around them. In short, this heady period of development encapsulates Alberta's spirit today—and the struggles that it continues to wrestle with.

The Railroad Opens the Plains

The year 1883 marked a major turning point for the Alberta area, and it ultimately proved decisive in the shaping of the future province's character. Until that time, trade across the continent was fractured and difficult. Trails like the Carlton Trail connected Fort Edmonton with points east, but passage west over the Rocky Mountains remained treacherous. Except for a trickle of materials in and out of Vancouver, little effective cross-continental trade existed. The building of the

Canadian Pacific Railway (CPR) during the 1880s changed things dramatically. Begun in 1881, within two years the CPR had reached from Montreal to Fort Calgary, built by the Northwest Mounted Police only six years earlier. On November 7, 1885, construction crews working from the east and west met at Craigellachie, British Columbia, driving in the last spike to connect Port Moody (and, in 1887, Vancouver) on the Pacific to the eastern seaboard.

The finishing of the transcontinental railway not only increased trade but also opened up land for settlers in the new District of Alberta that the government had carved out of the Northwest Territories in 1882. (The name honored Princess Louise Caroline Alberta, Queen Victoria's fourth daughter.) By the mid-1890s, the Canadian government had developed a plan for an almost exclusively agricultural west. For $10 settlers could buy a 160-acre homestead on the prairies and begin to farm. The main provisions of the government plan called for tenants to stay on the land for at least three years, break a certain amount of land per year, and build a house. This rather narrowly conceived development plan paid little attention to the need for towns, or to the rights of First Nations, Métis, and other peoples already settled in the area. Ultimately, says scholar and historian Pierre Berton,

> The prairies were to be settled by practical farmers; nobody else was wanted from overseas. City people, clerks, shopkeepers, and artisans were not to be considered. . . . The West would be a gigantic granary, tied to Central Canada by a ribbon of steel. The wheat would move east in ever-increasing quantities; the manufactured goods required by

■ *Steam-powered farm equipment aided in the Canadian government's desire to develop agriculture in the 1890s.*

■ *An immigrant farmer and his family try to make a living on Alberta's bleak plains region.*

Western farmers would fill up the empty freight cars on the return journey.[17]

To the government planners, the most desirable people were those from northern Europe—Scandinavia, Germany, Scotland, and Great Britain. Italians, Jews, blacks, and others were considered less desirable.[18] The government backed its homesteading plan with a public relations campaign that minimized the area's harsh climate, referring to winters as merely "brisk" when in fact the average daily low for the area around Calgary ranges from 9° to 12° F (−13° to −11° C) for the months of December, January, and February. The government also exaggerated how fast crops could grow in the area and failed to mention that some of the southern plains were too dry for most farming. The government did try to use zoning regulations to reserve areas with the richest soils for farming, leaving the remainder of the land for ranching. Grazing leases often went to rich and politically connected individuals, who established some of the country's largest ranches.

Life on the Homestead

In addition to the few thousand German, Irish, Scottish, and other immigrants who trickled into the Canadian plains, the newcomers also included white and black Americans. In the United States, much of the best farmland had been swallowed up or was selling for a premium, thus triggering Americans' interest in Canada. The Canadian government preferred to discourage American influence, but on the other hand it

■ Black Migration to Alberta

Black fur traders and black cowboys were occasionally spotted on the Canadian prairies as early as the 1870s. This was due in part to Canada's reputation as a tolerant and culturally diverse land—during America's Civil War, Canada East and Canada West (present-day Quebec and Ontario, respectively) had welcomed many blacks escaping slavery through the "underground railroad." Many of these early blacks of the prairies left striking impressions on people. In *The Blacks in Canada: A History*, historian Robin Winks describes John Ware, one of the most important black figures in the District of Alberta. Ware, says Winks, "became a legend in his lifetime after arriving in 1882. One of the finest riders in Alberta's range history, Ware died in 1905 when his horse fell with him, and he was honored by having a mountain, a creek, and a coulee named after him."

It was not until the first decade of the twentieth century, however, that blacks from the United States began to take a serious interest in settling on Canada's prairies. Favorable publicity about Alberta that appeared in Oklahoma in particular prompted more than one thousand blacks to migrate to Alberta from 1905 to 1911. These black settlers helped to establish such Alberta towns as Breton, Clyde, and Amber Valley. They accomplished this despite frequently having to deal with the type of discrimination that they had hoped to leave behind in the United States.

After initially accepting blacks, if not welcoming them, the Canadian government began to try to limit their immigration. For example, it began to subject blacks to rigorous, even absurd, physical examinations designed to keep many out of the country. The Canadian government also began to spread news stories in the United States about how Canada was "too cold" for blacks. These tactics had the desired effect of virtually ending black migration to Alberta for many decades after 1912.

■ *An artist's depiction of slaves escaping to Canada.*

found that Americans tended to bring money and thus economic power to the territory.

Instead of a paradise of cheap land and fast-growing crops, homesteaders in many areas found open prairies of grassland more suited for ranching, scorching hot summers, little rain, and brutal winters. Initially, farmers followed the government's desire—they raised mostly wheat as a main crop. But drought, grasshoppers and other pests, frosts, and diseases plagued the early wheat crops, and thousands of farmers suffered complete crop failures. So devastating was the initial failure at farming that as many as half the immigrants from the United States gave up their homesteads and headed back to their native soil. The remaining farmers learned to diversify by raising several types of field crops and incorporating dairy cows, pigs, and chickens into their farms.

The toughness and vigor prairie settlers needed to survive the harsh conditions spread throughout the territory and later the province. J.G. MacGregor, whose family came from Scotland and settled just south of Edmonton near the turn of the century, recalled the treacherous winter months, particularly in the early years. "When, one by one," he said, "the ears and tails of the cattle fall off from the frost, and those that live till spring are a sorry sight; the hay and then the straw gives out and you buy straw at fabulous prices and haul it for miles; when the snow is so deep that hay racks upset two or three times on the way home and when you get there you find two more cattle dead—that's how you measure a cold winter."[19]

Such living, though, helped the people of the western plains to develop their characteristically stubborn and gritty outlook. They realized that they were capable of enduring hardships unknown to fellow Canadians back east. In the years just prior to their acceptance into the Canadian federation, the people of present-day Alberta first began to assert an air of western superiority for their toughness and bravery against the elements.

Stability from Ranching

Like its farmers, the territory's ranchers felt a certain pride in their survival on the open plains. While many farmers were poor immigrants from distant places like Norway and Germany, ranchers typically came from far better-off backgrounds. "The aspiring rancher in western Canada typically

■ This National Historic Site in Longview, Alberta, commemorates the contribution of ranching to Alberta's development.

had both money and, in most cases, higher education and professional skills," according to Alberta's Heritage Community Foundation. "Some had come from the ranges of Montana and were already skilled ranch-hands, but just as many were British gentlemen—young, adventurous, and possessed of some financial means."[20]

Like farmers, ranchers were drawn by the promise of inexpensive land, but the ranchers also brought with them something the government desperately wanted on the open plains—financial and political stability. Land was leased cheaply to ranchers, and they were required to grow their herds consistently so that eventually there was one head of cattle for every 10 acres of land owned. The first cattle herd came to the Bow River area near Calgary in 1873 with Methodist minister John McDougall. The railroad stimulated the industry, and by the late 1880s ranching was well established, with four major companies owning nearly half the government-leased land in the territory. Beef became a major export for Alberta. The industry even provided important jobs for some native peoples who were making the transition to reservation life.

Ranchers brought much needed stability to the region because they were better able than farmers to survive financial crises and seemed more willing to stick to their new homes through the tough times. The Canadian government worked with some success to avoid the violence common in the U.S. West. Canada's ranchers, supported by the Northwest Mounted Police, which the Canadian government organized in 1873, helped establish some of the area's first towns.

Many ranchers were active politically, serving on early school boards and town governments.

Ultimately, the boom in large-scale ranching passed, as government policy encouraged more and more settlers to arrive and begin farming. But the town structures ranchers had built helped the territory through the first of two major economic expansions in the years from 1880 to 1914. In addition, the roots of those structures persisted, and much of Alberta's stability today can be traced to the efforts of early ranchers.

The heady, boom-and-bust spirit in Alberta had already taken root with the coming of the railroad, but the economic expansion associated with the Klondike Gold Rush of the late-1890s helped entrench it in the psyche of the people. During these times, cities grew, infrastructures developed, and people changed their lifestyles rapidly, only to meet difficulty at the end of the boom.

■ *Trading posts, like this one near the Saskatchewan River, sprang up along gold rush routes through Alberta.*

Last Stop Before Gold

The discovery of gold in the area of the Klondike River in present-day Yukon Territory in the summer of 1897 set off a gold rush that had far-reaching effects over the North American continent. Prospectors from across the United States and Canada made their way west and north, hoping for instant wealth. In Alberta, towns started by the first ranchers and farmers saw explosive growth, and Edmonton in particular became an outfitting stop on the trek north.

Beginning in 1898, Edmonton, originally a fort built to support the fur trade, was suddenly transformed into a lively little city whose population doubled in just two years. Though the "Klondike Trail" from Edmonton was not considered the main route to the Yukon (the vast majority of gold seekers arrived by sea at Skagway, Alaska, and journeyed inland from there), Edmonton promoted itself as the final take-off spot on the

"Back Door" or the "All-Canadian Route." This route was long and time-consuming, being by water over the Athabasca, Slave, and Mackenzie Rivers almost to the Arctic Ocean, and then overland to the Yukon. But the lure of gold was strong. An estimated sixteen hundred prospectors set out on the route. Fewer than half ever made it—most gave up rather than die during the effort—but the gold rush fever changed Edmonton's shape and character. New services included not only prosperous outfitters, but also a host of less reputable businesses, from saloons to houses of prostitution. When the gold rush subsided in the early 1900s, much of the retail structure as well as the rough-and-tumble character of Edmonton persisted.

The Territory Becomes a Province

The establishment of a ranching industry, the economic expansion brought on by the Klondike Gold Rush, and the ongoing migration to the prairies ultimately pushed the District of Alberta toward entrance into the confederation. Until that time Alberta, Saskatchewan, and other western districts (including the District of Athabasca, much of present-day northern Alberta) had been ruled from Ottawa. The expanding populations and growing number of towns strained government services, however, and it was time to consider full provincial status.

Only by being a province could Alberta hope to compete with other provinces for federal money. As historian Gerald Friesen has noted, the territories and districts did not stand on the same footing as the provinces. "To build new schools, control prairie fires, build roads, and license businesses," he notes, "the local administration required rapid adjustments in the federal subsidy. But such a change in the per capita grant from Ottawa, which lay at the heart of the federal-provincial system, inevitably roused expressions of righteous indignation from seven provincial premiers and threatened to drag on for years."[21]

Ultimately, the government responded to Alberta's expanding economy and population. In 1905, Alberta and Saskatchewan were officially separated from the Northwest Territories to create two new provinces.

Unfortunately for the people of Alberta, provincial status came at a price. The federal government decided to keep control of the provinces' forests, government lands, and other public domains. This was in stark contrast to the government's policy with other provinces. For example, when British Columbia became a province in 1871, the new provincial gov-

■ Carving Out Alberta's Borders

The entrance of Alberta into the Dominion of Canada is a classic study in partisan politics. During the first years of the twentieth century, the federal government began to respond to the obvious need for people in the western parts of the country to have greater local control. Wilfrid Laurier, who served as Canada's prime minister from 1896 to 1911, was a member of the Liberal Party. It was the Conservative Party, however, that was most forcefully backing provincial status for the prairies, in part because the acknowledged political leader of the prairie area was Frederick Haultain, a Conservative. Laurier wanted to keep the political power that would be embodied in a single, large western province out of Conservative Party hands. So Laurier worked to create two provinces—Alberta and Saskatchewan—divided along the 110° line of longitude. He then appointed Regina and Edmonton as the two provisional capitals, and he placed Liberal leaders in charge of the provisional governments that would call the first elections. These actions meant that the federal two-party system was entrenched in both provinces, and in the elections both provinces voted for Liberal governments.

ernment was granted control over the vast forests that cover approximately 60 percent of its land. These forests, as well as mineral rights, have ever since provided large sums of money to the British Columbia government, through leases of the land and sales of resource-related products.

But when it came time for Alberta and Saskatchewan to become provinces, the federal government was much less generous. Keeping the land rights accomplished several objectives. It allowed Ottawa to maintain tighter control over land leasing and sales, thus helping them control immigration patterns. Federal control also allowed Ottawa to sell or lease huge tracts of land to giant ranching companies and other industries in exchange for political favors. Such patronage was used to assert and retain power over the provincial governments.

This federal selfishness, not reversed until 1930, had at least one long-lasting side effect: it cemented Alberta's view of itself as separate from—and better than—"the East." It caused the citizens of newly minted Alberta to look on eastern Canadians, ignorant of the struggles the prairie people faced, with suspicion. Berton notes that the Alberta newspapers of the day railed against the East: "The [Calgary] *Herald* saw the West as a distinctive entity, its very newness an asset, unshackling the people from the hidebound East."[22] It was not until

■ Population Wars

Edmonton and Calgary have competed with each other at least since the former was chosen over the latter as provincial capital in 1905. One form of that competition has been population. Since the early 1900s each city has viewed population growth as a source of civic pride. Census figures are thus closely scrutinized—and frequently contested.

In 1907, the census said that Edmonton and Calgary each had about eleven thousand people. The Calgary newspapers accused the "Eastern census takers" of being biased, and city officials put fierce pressure on the federal government to revise the figures. In response, the government did revise the figures and gave Calgary credit for fourteen thousand residents, at the same time reducing Edmonton's population by several hundred. In 1912 Edmonton struck back by successfully incorporating into it the neighboring city of Strathcona, across the North Saskatchewan River. The new double-city's official population soared to more than fifty thousand. Meanwhile, Calgary languished at a mere forty-three thousand. Indignant Calgarians insisted that an "accurate" count would show that the population was, in fact, higher.

The population competition continues to this day. Calgary rejoiced recently when the 2001 census figures showed that it had overtaken Edmonton in the previous five years to become the province's largest city. In fact, Calgary accounted for almost half of the province's greater than 10 percent growth in population from 1996 to 2001, which was the highest growth rate among Canada's provinces and territories. The most recent census also determined that the 170-mile-long (275-kilometer) Calgary–Edmonton corridor includes six of the twenty-five fastest-growing municipalities in Canada.

the province developed as an economic power later in the twentieth century that "the East" truly began to appreciate the importance of Alberta and its people to the confederation.

Cattle Drive a Real Estate Boom

From 1906 to the start of World War I, the expansion of railway services and farming drove a booming economy that thrived more and more on the sale of land. City pride and the desire to snap up land led cities like Edmonton and Calgary to dramatically expand their borders. Calgary annexed land voraciously, growing from 1,600 acres in 1884 to 26,000 acres by 1912. The population swelled as well, as people followed the railroads into the cities or sought farmland or ranch land near the railroads and cities. Still, with the flood of people coming into the province for railway, ranching, and manufacturing work,

Alberta maintained its rugged, freewheeling nature, in large part because of the nature of the expansion.

The real estate boom was driven primarily by the increasing number of railroads, which in turn was driven by the cattle industry. The prosperous times, says Berton, were marked by nearly absurd land sales. At the height of the real estate market in 1912, lots in Calgary that had been $2,000 in 1905 sold for $300,000, and prospective landowners had no qualms about paying inflated prices for land they had never seen.

But the real estate industry could not have charged on without the cattle industry. With its supporting industries of stockyards, tanneries, and transportation, cattle accounted for 25 percent of Alberta's manufacturing industry by 1911. In this time period, important Western cultural markers, like the Calgary Stampede (1912) and other rodeos, sprang up and persist to this day.

Edmonton's success was not as swift as Calgary's, but Edmonton brought in two transcontinental railways (the Canadian Northern in 1905 and the Grand Trunk Pacific in 1909) and enjoyed the support of surrounding farmlands to provide wholesale and retail goods. Because of its landholdings, Edmonton's economy grew quickly, as the lumber and brick industries became more important.

Post-Boom Bust

Such expansion, though, could not last, and the challenges that awaited Alberta became much like the early challenges of taming the prairies against the difficult elements. In 1914, the start

■ *Large grain elevators located alongside railroad tracks are the modern-day result of Alberta's early agricultural expansion.*

■ *Railway workers stand by a locomotive belonging to Alberta's Grand Trunk Pacific line.*

of World War I curtailed the real estate expansion, as industry and resources turned toward supporting the war effort. In addition, several huge crop failures between 1910 and 1920 impoverished many farmers. Those farmers who managed to thrive during the war did so because of their ability to grow wheat, which was desperately needed on the front. When the war ended and these farmers needed to quickly diversify into other crops, they suffered economically again. In the 1920s, many farmers joined labor groups in protesting government favoritism toward big business, especially the grain and railway companies that seemed to profit during good times and bad.

The Great Depression that began in 1929 deeply hurt the farmers and laborers of Alberta and reduced Alberta's stature in the confederation. Alberta's population shrank by more than forty thousand during the 1930s as residents sought jobs in Toronto, Montreal, and elsewhere. Only with the rise of the oil industry, started by the major 1947 oil discovery near Edmonton, did Alberta begin the climb to the prominence it enjoys today.

Diverse Newcomers Arrive

The early vision that the Canadian government had of Alberta as a province of northern European farmers was never realistic, and the area has long attracted a diverse population. For example, thousands of Chinese came to help build the Canadian Pacific Railway in the 1880s. Chinatowns developed in Calgary, Edmonton, Lethbridge, and Medicine Hat. Although these Chinese faced discrimination, and laws were passed to slow their immigration, by the first decades of the twentieth century they had become an important and permanent political and cultural influence on the province.

In the south, Mormon settlers found Alberta to be a respite from the persecution they faced in much of the United States. Mormons, despised for their practice of polygamy in their early years, helped settle many areas in the south, particularly Cardston and other surrounding towns.

Other ethnic groups and nationalities found their way to Alberta, as well, during the period of rapid settlement. Significant immigrant populations came from Japan, Norway, Iceland, and Ukraine. Even with such diversity and economic success, many groups suffered in varying degrees during the migration time. Some, like blacks, Italians, Jews, and Chinese, faced hostility and discrimination. Others, like the native peoples and Métis, struggled just to maintain their cultural identities. First Nations and Métis peoples who had become accustomed to the nomadic life suddenly found themselves

■ *An Indian woman and child sit amidst their barren farmland in Alberta's arid region.*

forced to farm land that often was too dry or was otherwise unsuitable for agriculture. Many First Nations peoples lived in abject poverty.

Métis peoples, without even the structure of the reservations, suffered even more. Many did not understand the government's land scrip programs, and others refused to accept money the government offered. Some Métis became poverty-stricken wanderers. The Canadian government had accepted Manitoba (much smaller in size than today's province) as a Métis-led province in 1870, but settlers continued to flood into it and displace Métis. The Métis leader Louis Riel had been forced to flee Manitoba in 1870 after a conflict with the federal government. When he returned to lead a Métis rebellion in 1885 he was captured and executed. Métis fortunes suffered further in the aftermath of Riel's death. While some Métis peoples learned ranching or heavy industry, many others struggled. Partly out of a desire to find acceptance by their government, Métis as well as First Nations peoples served admirably in World War I, but upon returning home much of the struggle continued.

A Century of Change

Alberta in the years following the turn of the twentieth century was a province undergoing rapid change. In one generation, hundreds of thousands of people from around the world settled on the open prairies and ranges and struggled to survive. Their grit and drive helped make up the spirit of the West, though Western openness did not extend to all. Many ethnic groups, as well as First Nations and Métis peoples, battled persistent poverty and relentless discrimination. Even so, all these groups have survived, and today their problems and their successes are part of the identity of the modern-day province.

Life in Alberta Today

I n 1947, prospectors discovered a large oil field in Leduc south of Edmonton. This is often considered a pivotal date for the province but it was preceded by decades of related energy development. Both oil and natural gas had been discovered in fields southwest of Calgary by the 1930s. These findings had attracted petroleum companies to the area and Calgary had its first two oil refineries prior to the start of World War II. The area was also well established as a coal producer, with its first shipment out of Lethbridge way back in 1886.

The 1947 discovery, however, changed the face of Alberta. It occurred during the postwar boom years and inspired more aggressive energy exploration within the province. Prominent new discoveries were made during the 1950s and 1960s, including the Pembina field south of Edmonton that was hailed as the largest oil field in Canada. More oil companies poured into Alberta, and particularly into Calgary, bringing with them tens of thousands of jobs in administration, extraction, transportation, and pipeline construction.

The energy boom has had major effects on the daily lives of many Alberta residents. Moreover, in recent years the province has grown more and more diverse, and with that diversity comes a wider range of lifestyles and living standards.

Energy Millionaires and Small Farmers

In 1935, over half of Alberta's wealth came from agriculture while only 10 percent came from mining, including oil. By the late 1970s, the trend had reversed—over half the province's wealth came from mining, particularly oil, while agriculture

■ *A large lake of oil surrounds a well at the oil field in Leduc, Alberta.*

contributed less than 15 percent to the total. Today Alberta is not only Canada's principal oil producer, if the province were a country it would rank as the world's eighteenth-largest oil producer. Alberta is also a world-class natural gas producer and exporter, and contains approximately 70 percent of Canada's coal reserves. The energy boom has driven Alberta to the forefront of Canada as an economic—if not yet political—power.

While oil and natural gas revenues have brought high-tech industries and modern attitudes to the expanding cities, and created what is probably Canada's largest class of millionaires, many communities are still rooted in the traditional ways of farming, ranching, and logging. Farm communities, for example, are bound by nightly social functions, a stark contrast to the nightly entertainment, theaters, sports, and other activities found in Alberta's major cities. First Nations and Métis peoples balance old traditions with new technology and government programs.

Though diverse in homes, jobs, and backgrounds, to a great degree Albertans still manage to share a unique mix of qualities, including civic and cultural pride, an entrepreneurial spirit, a stubborn willingness to endure nature's challenges, and a suspicion of "the East."

Life in the Big Cities

Edmonton and Calgary are Alberta's two biggest cities, with their metropolitan areas collectively housing more than half of the province's population. Both cities have grown explosively since the 1950s and 1960s energy boom. These two cities rival each other and compete to attract workers, visitors, and university students. Alberta, particularly Edmonton and Calgary, "was Canada's Cinderella in the post-1940s decades. . . . Nowhere was growth so rapid, the increase in wealth so obvious, the atmosphere of confidence so palpable,"[23] notes Friesen.

Much of that same attitude drives Edmonton and Calgary today. Both cities continue to expand, and the people in each live diverse lifestyles and enjoy some of Alberta's highest prosperity. Alberta city life, typified by that found in its two key cities, is marked by a progressive spirit nevertheless tied to a western heritage. The people differ individually, but they generally enjoy an active lifestyle, the benefits of employment and education, and the comforts of nearby shopping and leisure activities.

Edmonton: The Capital City

Edmonton's character as a boomtown has been reinforced a number of times since the city first flourished briefly during the Klondike Gold Rush era. Today, Edmonton continues to

■ *An aerial view of downtown Edmonton, Alberta.*

thrive on the energy boom of recent decades. More residents of Edmonton work in oil, gas, and other energy industries than in any other industry. While Calgary hosts more of the industry's office workers, Edmonton has the edge in hands-on laborers—the workers who build and maintain the industry's heavy machinery and pipelines. Other laborers work in area refineries and processing plants. Of course, Edmonton also has many white-collar engineers and researchers who help develop the techniques, equipment, and methods for extracting oil.

As has long been true, Edmonton is supported by a strong agricultural and manufacturing community. While Edmonton laborers process and manufacture one-third of Alberta's food and drinks, other workers are employed in the pharmaceutical, paper manufacturing, and chemical industries. The city also has active timber, transportation, and biotechnology industries. As the capital city for Alberta, Edmonton is the site of the provincial government and many of its various agencies and branches. In addition, city planners have worked feverishly to expand Edmonton's high-tech business base. Finally, Edmonton boasts more retail space than in any other Canadian city.

■ *Amongst numerous other attractions, the enormous West Edmonton Mall features a pool with submarines and a pirate's ship.*

Beyond business and work, Edmonton residents enjoy a variety of leisure and recreational activities. Residents and visitors alike flock to the West Edmonton Mall, billed as the world's largest indoor shopping and amusement center. Those who tire of shopping in its eight hundred stores can swim in a wave pool, see a dolphin show, play miniature golf, or go for a ride on the world's largest indoor roller coaster. Edmonton residents are also likely to take advantage of health clubs, regatta clubs, community softball and hockey teams, and other community-oriented activities. In short, Edmonton residents enjoy most of the benefits of city living found elsewhere, including diverse job opportunities, quality educational opportunities, and leisure and retail services that rank with much of the world's best.

■ *Hailed as the energy capital of Canada, Calgary, Alberta, is an important economic center.*

Calgary: Energy Capital of Canada

Even more so than Edmonton, Calgary is the energy capital of Canada. And while there is plenty of industry to claim that title, Calgary residents pride themselves on their diversity—in work, education, and community activities. Just one hour east of the Rockies, Calgary now numbers close to 1 million residents, and it claims the highest percentage of people in any Canadian city with at least some post-secondary education—58 percent. In fact, the city boasts a higher concentration of workers in science, engineering, or mathematics positions than any other Canadian city. That degree of education is reflected in the numerous professional industries thriving in the city, and it is a source of pride for residents.

Like Edmonton, much of Calgary's labor force works in the oil and energy industries and in manufacturing, doing everything from heavy construction to management and engineering. Because more than 80 percent of Canada's oil and natural gas producers are based in Calgary, workers specialize particularly in oil engineering and construction, natural gas compression and transmission, and geological analysis and data processing. Many other area residents help to manufacture heavy machinery for the energy industries. Still others produce clothes, foods and beverages, wood products, and printing and publishing products. Further, many Calgary residents remain tied to the vocations that built the city—ranching and farming. The city offers numerous opportunities in the fields of cattle, grain, and wheat processing, ranging from setting up livestock shows to marketing food.

Beyond the oil, manufacturing, and food industries, a multitude of workers have taken positions at the more than one thousand high-tech companies in the Calgary area. They help develop telecommunications and information management systems, fiber optic networks, and digital entertainment systems. Calgary workers have played a key role in making and donating thousands of computers to Alberta classrooms, thus helping students across the province learn about the most recent technology.

Outside of work and school, Calgary residents enjoy parks, recreation, and shopping. The city is home to museums, a historic park, a zoo, and botanical gardens. Many Calgarians utilize hundreds of fitness clubs, gymnasiums, tennis courts, and swimming pools to stay in shape and relax. Skiers are attracted to the Calgary Olympic Park, built originally for the 1988 Winter Olympic Games but now open for tourism and recreational use. Beyond all that, numerous parks and nearby reservoirs provide plenty of opportunities for boating, hiking, and camping.

Rural Life on the Plains and Parklands

Alberta's farms and rural communities stand in stark contrast to the rapidly expanding major cities. While modern technology is prevalent and the farming and ranching industries have changed dramatically over the last 100 years, the communities themselves remain largely devoted to local events and concerns. Rural communities are often brought together by unity-building traditions. While these may lack the large-scale hoopla of big-city celebrations, small-town festivals and community events often involve practically the entire local population. Many Alberta towns were established predominantly by a single ethnic group. Although these towns are often more diverse today, ethnic traditions and festivals are still cherished.

Before the energy boom in Alberta, rural life was particularly challenging. Small towns in much of the province faced tough times and were losing population because they were dependent on farming and thus liable to suffer from the effects of drought, low product prices, and other economic and natural hazards. The oil and gas industries have profoundly transformed life in rural Alberta. While the communities remain tight-knit and quiet, the modern energy industries have brought jobs and stability to even the smallest towns. Towns like Cold Lake in the east claim an oil sands plant as their key economic base, while towns like High Level in the north com-

■ The Oil Sands

Once known as tar sands, oil sands are deposits of a heavy, sticky form of crude oil (bitumen) that naturally occur in a mixture of sand, water, and clay. Alberta has more oil sands deposits than anywhere else in the world with the exception of Venezuela. The upgraded crude oil Alberta processes from its oil sands deposits account for about 40 percent of the province's total oil production.

Producing gasoline and diesel fuels from oil sands is an expensive process. Thousands of workers are involved in mining the sands, processing the bitumen, and getting the finished products to markets. Oil sands are often mined at surface pits, with up to two tons of oil sands being needed to ultimately produce a single barrel of oil. The thick, black bitumen must be extracted from the sand and water before it can be processed into lighter crude oil. The sand can then be replaced in the mining pits.

The Athabasca Oil Sands in the area of Fort McMurray, 230 miles (370 kilometers) north of Edmonton, have the most bitumen of any deposit in Alberta—1.7 trillion barrels of bitumen, which, with current technology, could be processed into 300 billion barrels of oil. In essence, the Athabasca Oil Sands contain more oil than all of the known oil deposits in Saudi Arabia. Given that Canada has only 4.5 billion barrels of oil in its reserves, it is clear that Alberta's oil sands will grow in economic importance as Canada continues to rely on the province for energy and revenue.

bine exploratory drilling with other services to support their economy.

Located in east-central Alberta, the tiny (population 250) village of Alliance seems a prime example of the industry effects. Town officials boast that the local economy has been reinvigorated by the oil industry. Supporting the energy industry are two manufacturing and welding establishments and a supplies, parts, and maintenance store. But energy does not stand alone: Agriculture is still deeply rooted in rural Alberta, and the two welding shops compete for agricultural business—welding corrals, fences, and gates—as well.

Although the small towns that claim oil and gas as key industries often list agriculture alongside those industries, today's farm economy has shifted such that individual farm operators now own huge amounts of land so that they have sufficient crop diversity to remain profitable. In addition to bringing in 30 percent of the country's wheat sales, Alberta farmers account for the sale of 38 percent of the country's barley, 34 percent of its canola, 48 percent of its hay, and 20 percent of its dry peas. Farmers now oversee larger amounts of land than ever before in Alberta, and the costs of managing large pieces of land can be extraordinary—a combine, used for threshing and harvesting grain, can run $175,000. Fertilizer, weed killer, and other chemicals and fuels needed to operate an industrial farm can run thousands of dollars per year. Many farmers compensate with automated feeding systems, electronic monitoring devices on farm equipment, and satellite and computer communications to take quick advantage of market developments.

Ranching has also become a corporate industry, with much of the Alberta industry dominated by large organizations overseeing huge operations. Owners of smaller, traditional ranches sometimes supplement their income with tourism services that allow visitors, for example, to participate on the ranch.

Beyond oil, farming, and ranching, the forestry industry supports many small-town families. The industry has important locations across Alberta—it's the province's third-largest industry and employs a total of fifty thousand residents—but most lumbering is concentrated in the western and northern forests. For instance, High Level, a small town in the northwest corner of the province, is a major distribution center for timber and processed wood products because of its location in Footner Lake Forest. Footner Lake is Alberta's largest forest, covering almost 30,000 square miles (77,700 square kilometers). Even so, recent years have not been kind to the highly

■ *Ranchers drive cattle on one of Alberta's many large cattle ranches.*

competitive timber industry. Prices have fallen and many workers have lost their jobs.

Education in Alberta

Alberta provides mandatory schooling for all children aged six to nineteen who have not completed twelfth grade. A majority of approximately 57 percent attend public schools; most of the private schools are religious, particularly Catholic, schools. Alberta provides partial funding to private schools (as do a number of other Canadian provinces) but is leading the way in Canada in establishing charter schools. Alberta's public school teachers are the highest paid of any province, and the province ranks third in the country in student-to-teacher ratios with 16.8 students to every teacher. Those students who attend private schools often make the choice to gain special instruction in an area such as religion or French language.

The province's public schools offer diverse instruction in various topics. Students participate in sports, second-language learning (they particularly study French), and a variety of other activities such as drama and art. Technology has become central to many classrooms, particularly in the city school systems—some children write for classroom websites as early as the first grade. Students in public schools generally have fully computerized libraries and often have networked computers within their classrooms. In Edmonton and Calgary, many students participate in specialized schooling, attending classes

■ Alberta's schools offer many learning opportunities including field trips to the province's national parks.

■ Alberta's Hutterian Minority

Hutterians, or Hutterites, are members of a Christian religious sect begun in Europe in the sixteenth century. Like two other sectarian groups, the Mennonites and the Amish, Hutterians pursue a simple lifestyle and have retained traditional clothing and customs. Hutterians practice adult baptism, oppose war, and hold all things in common, thus eliminating personal property. Alberta and Canada's other prairie provinces account for about two-thirds of the current Hutterian world population of about twenty-five thousand.

Persecuted by Americans during World War I for their pacifist beliefs, many Hutterians migrated from villagelike farms in the Dakotas to the plains of Alberta. Here they started dozens of settlements, mostly in the areas of Cardston in the south or just northeast of Calgary. In the difficult early years, Hutterians erected buildings, dug wells, and bought agricultural machinery and livestock in order to establish their communal culture. They have since struck a deal with the Canadian government whereby they are exempt from military service, public office, and state education (they supervise their own education). The agreement has not always been followed, and Alberta's Hutterians at various times have been persecuted for their practices. Today, however, the Hutterian farm settlements (typically made up of a dozen or so families and about one hundred individuals) remain deeply rooted in traditional communal living.

with a focused art core, sports alternative curriculum, or special language training ranging from Arabic to Mandarin.

Schooling in the rural communities varies widely. Many rural schools are private or religious schools designed to meet the needs of the local culture. While no one school or community is typical, it is common for school buses to drive out to students' houses in the morning and meet children where their properties cross county roads. Even tiny schools must accommodate younger and older learners alike, often from different language backgrounds. For instance, Neudorf Colony School in southern Alberta teaches in German and English and deals with a handful of children from various backgrounds, including Hutterian. The Hutterians learn to read and write High German in German school, and they begin learning English when they enter first grade.

Other rural schools benefit from high technology. At Ochre Park School in Redwater near the North Saskatchewan River, children have access to an art room, computer lab, and kitchen, and students help write copy for the school website, draw and scan pictures, and post information about the town.

Alberta has sixteen public colleges, two technical institutes, four universities, and seven private colleges. These are open to a variety of students depending on the institution and the background of the applicant. Public colleges tend to offer two- and four-year degree programs, and their admission requirements are not as selective as larger universities like the University of Calgary and the University of Alberta in Edmonton.

The University of Calgary is the most research-intensive university in Alberta, and its more than twenty thousand students study issues such as the environment, petrochemical engineering, law and the family, and the humanities. In addition, Mount Royal College, servicing more than forty thousand students, provides a wide range of degree programs and continuing education opportunities. Beyond regular colleges and universities, the Southern Alberta Institute of Technology and DeVry Institute offer programs in technical trades and in business and technology. More than forty thousand students attend, and job placement after these programs exceeds 90 percent.

Life on the Reserves

Many First Nations peoples have blended into the communities around them and thus have much of the same lifestyle found in the towns and big cities of Alberta. In addition, many of those living within cities have begun looking back to their heritage and finding ways to connect to their past. Even so, many others remain on reserves (reservations) or settlements, balancing traditional lifestyles with modern technology and lifestyles. Canada's 1996 census counted approximately one hundred twenty thousand First Nations people living in Alberta. Of those, slightly more than 50 percent live on reserves.

First Nations tribes typically control hiring and curriculum development in the schools, with the support and funding of the federal government. While such schools help students learn everything from mathematics to tribal traditions, education on reserves remains a persistent problem. For instance, of the two thousand people of the Little Red River Cree Nation, located in two reserves east of High Level, more than 55 percent over age fifteen have less than a ninth-grade education. Only 6 percent of the population has any university schooling, with a smaller percentage completing degrees.

Beyond schooling, people on the reserves try to balance traditional living with the demands of modern society. But doing so can be difficult. Life on the reserves is often a challenge

■ *Native Canadians demonstrate their heritage at a cultural event in Calgary.*

at best, and poverty-stricken at worst. Many reserves depend on farming as their main economic activity, but often agriculture cannot sustain the whole settlement. So residents of reserves have learned to survive through other means. For instance, while many on the Blood Indian Reserve southwest of Lethbridge farm wheat and other crops, others are involved in drapery making, crafts, silk screening, plumbing and heating, cattle operations, and other jobs. The reserve population of six thousand is served by a grocery store, a gas station, and a restaurant.

The Siksika Nation on the Blackfoot Reserve enjoys greater development, perhaps in part from the relatively close proximity of Calgary 40 miles (65 kilometers) to the west. The reserve has a seniors lodge, a college, several schools, a sports center, a golf course, and a mall. The Siksika Nation's industries include tourism, farming, ranching, and clothes manufacturing.

A Renewed Sense of Heritage

Despite the many challenges facing First Nations and Métis peoples, both on reserves and in the cities, the native peoples of Alberta are finding ways to keep their rich heritage alive, thus contributing to the overall diversity and spirit of Alberta. In this effort, the First Nations and Métis peoples are not alone. In their daily lives and in their celebrations and art forms, Albertans of all descents define themselves and look back on their heritage, while embracing new and classical arts.

Arts and Culture

A s Alberta grows in population and in national prominence, its artistic and cultural expressions grow richer and more diverse. Across the province, Albertans love to celebrate their heritage, whether it is through western rodeos or through traditional crafts. But Albertans have embraced more than just the symbols and art forms of their past—many are actively engaged in classical arts, like music and ballet, or are expressing themselves through radio, television, and film. Deep-rooted in the culture, as well, is a love for sports of all varieties including ice hockey, football, skiing, and curling. Alberta supports professional teams in a number of these sports, and all of them make for great recreation and community gathering. In short, the spirit of the West is alive and well in Alberta's arts and culture, even while Albertans embrace the most current types of recreation and entertainment.

Celebrating a Wild West Heritage

First and foremost, Albertans love to celebrate their heritage. For many, that heritage goes back to the nineteenth century and the pioneering "Spirit of the West" era of prospecting and cattle ranching. Across Alberta, various rodeos and western-style festivals give the people of Alberta a chance to congregate and remember what sets them apart from much of the rest of Canada. In smaller cities like Red Deer, located about halfway between Edmonton and Calgary, festivals celebrate rural roots while providing much that attracts city dwellers. Red Deer's five-day Westerner Days extravaganza every July, for example, opens with a parade and features concerts, carnival rides, and chuck wagon races. Ranchers bring their prize stock to the many agricultural pavilions to compete in contests. For residents and tourists alike, it is a time to have fun while learning about Alberta's early settlers as well as its modern farmers and ranchers.

Even small towns often host one- or two-day festivals. In Alliance, the annual July 1st Sports Day festival opens with a community pancake breakfast and is followed by a parade down Main Street, activities throughout the day, and a fireworks display at night.

The most memorable and spectacular celebrations of western heritage, however, happen in Edmonton and Calgary. In early November, Edmonton hosts the Canadian Finals Rodeo, the rodeo with Canada's richest prize money. More than ninety thousand spectators turn out to watch rodeo events including saddlebronc riding, bull riding, bareback riding, calf roping, and ladies barrel racing. The celebration also includes the crowning of Miss Rodeo Canada, bullfighting, and crowd-pleasing clowning.

During the same week, Edmonton hosts Farmfair International, Canada's foremost purebred livestock show and sale. More than twelve hundred farmers bring some six thousand animals, including cattle, sheep, pigs, and llamas, to compete in a livestock showcase. Farmfair is also part trade show, allowing farmers, ranchers, suppliers, and others in the agricul-

■ *Horses, wagons, and their drivers go head-to-head at the chuck wagon races during Westerner Days in Red Deer, Alberta.*

tural business an opportunity to make contacts and promote their products.

If one event were named as the defining celebration of Alberta's Western heritage, it would have to be the Calgary Stampede. Begun as a "Wild West Show" and rodeo in 1912, the stampede is now an annual, city-wide, ten-day event that in recent years has attracted more than 1 million people in total attendance. In its early days, as it does today, says Berton, the stampede showed that "Westerners *were* different, like Texans. There was a swagger here, a looseness, a gambling spirit, the kind of devil-may-care style that was the attraction of the chuck wagon races."[24] In addition to wildly popular and highly competitive chuck wagon races, held since 1923, the stampede offers numerous concerts (some of which feature country music and pop stars), tractor pulls, rodeos, light shows, talent contests, livestock competitions, nightly fireworks, and many other events. The full festival is so large that it has been called "The Greatest Outdoor Show on Earth."

■ *A rodeo rider competes at the Calgary Stampede.*

Native Arts and Crafts

Of course, there is more to Alberta's heritage than the cowboy spirit of settlers. First Nations and Métis peoples honor their heritage year-round through crafts, dances, and art. Many of the reserve residents earn money from sales of traditional art and crafts. In addition, aboriginal peoples have started many societies to celebrate their heritage. For example, the Edmonton Métis Cultural Dance Society performs at various events in Alberta, and it hosts dancing, singing, and talent contests. Reflecting their mixed heritage, the Métis perform dances with a First Nations flavor to the accompaniment of European fiddle tunes, jigs, and reels.

First Nations peoples are well known for large cultural gatherings, as well, that commemorate traditional ceremonies. For example, the Siksika Nation on the Blackfoot Reserve holds an annual powwow, a festival celebrating the nation's heritage. The event typically lasts three days in

■ *A Siksika Indian performs a Native hoop dance at the annual powwow on the Blackfoot Reserve.*

mid-August and features drumming competitions, traditional dance contests, and native arts and crafts displays. A princess is crowned and Siksika leaders make speeches.

Beyond that, First Nations peoples produce distinctive artwork that is sought by museums and galleries across Alberta. The well-known Glenbow Museum in downtown Calgary, for instance, prides itself on its collection of native art. The collection ranges from the historic to the modern, and it covers themes such as the importance of the land, the connections to ancestors, and the issues facing native peoples today.

First Nations peoples, like Albertans in general, feel a deep connection to their heritage. Their artistic expressions in dance, art, and ceremony are rooted in tradition and keep alive much of the past. But Alberta's cultural scene encompasses far more.

From Ballet to Alternative Theater

As Alberta grows, it increasingly supports the arts, from classical dance to alternative theater. Calgary and Edmonton, in particular, host numerous professional arts companies, such as the Alberta Ballet and the Edmonton Symphony Orchestra, that bring the performing arts to a large and appreciative audience.

Formed in 1966, the Calgary-based Alberta Ballet is the province's premier ballet company. The company tours the province, Canada, and North America, performing classics like the annual *Nutcracker* as well as modern dances. The ballet also collaborates with the University of Calgary to offer interested students a degree in dance. In addition, the ballet runs a school that helps aspiring professionals develop their skills and prepare for public performances.

The fifty-six-musician Edmonton Symphony Orchestra (ESO) recently celebrated its fiftieth birthday. It performs the classics, Broadway hits, and modern-day compositions throughout the year. Perhaps the highlight of the orchestra's year is the five-day Enbridge Symphony Under the Sky, an outdoor, end-of-summer music festival the ESO organizes and holds in Edmonton's Hawrelak Park. In addition to performing each night, as part of the festival the ESO promotes donations to the local food bank and hosts a run for charity. The ESO also takes an active role in teaching music and music

■ Modern Native Art of Jane Ash Poitras

Jane Ash Poitras was born in 1951 in Fort Chipewyan, Alberta, into a mixed Chipewyan and Cree heritage. When Poitras was five, her mother's death led to Poitras being adopted by a German Canadian couple and raised in Edmonton. Her upbringing over the next two decades ignored her First Nations' background. After earning a degree in microbiology from the University of Alberta, Poitras decided to reconnect with her native heritage and make art her full-time study. She went to Columbia University in New York to earn a Masters in Fine Arts degree in printmaking but then returned to Alberta, where she currently has a studio in Edmonton.

Poitras is noted for a mixed-media, expressionistic approach that uses native motifs in dreamlike combinations. Much of her work focuses on the effects of colonial rule on native cultures and the resiliency of First Nations peoples. "She firmly believes that her work as an artist can assist in reestablishing a common pride and identity for North America's first peoples as well as providing a greater understanding of First Nations culture to all who view her art," notes the North Vancouver, B.C.–based Artists for Kids Trust. Poitras's art has been exhibited at the Canadian Culture Center in Paris, at the Glenbow Museum, and at the Hamburg Art Academy in Germany, among other places.

An oil painter from Scotland enjoys a funded three-month residency at the Banff Centre for the Arts.

appreciation to Alberta's young people. The Adopt-a-Player program pairs orchestra members with teachers and students in elementary schools and helps them compose an original piece of music.

Edmonton also hosts the largest alternative theater festival in North America. The celebrated Fringe Theatre Festival is an eleven-day event that draws more than half a million people every August. More than 150 groups of artists perform in theaters, performance spaces, and on the streets of Edmonton's historic Old Strathcona district.

Public Support for the Arts

As one of Canada's wealthiest provinces, Alberta has in recent years been able to provide significant public support for the performing arts. The Alberta Foundation for the Arts (AFA), a provincial agency established in 1991, uses funds derived from lottery revenues to enhance artistic development across the province. The foundation supports artists, writers, and filmmakers through grants and scholarships. Foundation services help artists connect to each and sell or exhibit their work. In addition, the AFA provides funding to support professional arts companies, public art galleries, and traveling exhibitions. For instance, a recent four-month exhibit called Rural Route showcased the work (some of it actually purchased by the AFA) of sculptors, painters, photographers, and others who had captured the rich, diverse Alberta landscape.

Another successful AFA program funds six arts-based summer schools with names like Youthwrite and Dramaworks. Alberta's artists can also take advantage of AFA scholarships to attend the renowned Banff Centre for the Arts. Located in the picturesque Banff National Park, the center offers multidisciplinary programs in film, video, audio/sound/music, interactive media, and photography. Many of the center's artists participate in the annual three-week Banff Arts Festival, a popular summer attraction that has run for more than seventy years. Artists, actors, dancers, and musicians enact plays, display art, and perform aboriginal dances, and academics lecture on art and modern literary theory.

A Center for Writing and Publishing

Writers are also finding Alberta a prime spot for publishing scholarly and popular work. Both the University of Calgary and the University of Alberta operate independent publishing houses. The University of Alberta publishes books on a wide range of topics, but they particularly specialize in the Canadian West, native studies, and natural and earth sciences. The University of Calgary focuses in particular on the Canadian and American West, experimental works, and international books.

Outside of university and scholarly publishing, many presses in Alberta publish books on topics that range from history to cowboy poetry. For example, Calgary's Red Deer Press is increasingly successfully handling numerous subjects but still focusing much of its attention on the province. Its publications have won numerous awards in and out of Alberta, and titles include Alberta-centered material like *The Food Lover's Guide to Alberta* and *A Pocket Guide to Reptiles and Amphibians of Alberta*.

In addition, Alberta has its own writers' guild and book publishers' organizations where writers, publishers, and illustrators connect with each other, share industry information,

■ French-Canadian Writer Georges Bugnet

More than twenty years after his death at age 101 in 1981, the legacy of Georges Bugnet is honored by the Alberta Writers Guild with the award that bears his name: the Georges Bugnet Award for Novel. Bugnet was born, raised, and educated in France. He came to Manitoba in 1904 and a year later, after the birth of his first son, he moved to St. Albert, Alberta. Eventually, he and his family settled near Lac Majeau, northwest of Edmonton.

Bugnet is best known for the novel *La Forêt (The Forest)*, which explored life in the woods and the effects of nature on human behavior. Bugnet also published numerous poems, articles, and reports, in both French and English publications, and he edited the Alberta French paper *l'Union*. But Bugnet was a multitalented "Renaissance man," and his writing was hardly his sole accomplishment. A skillful botanist, Bugnet cross-pollinated seeds to develop the Lagoda pine. He also crossed a double wild rose from Russia with the single Alberta type to make the Thérèse Bugnet rose (named after his sister). Because of Bugnet's efforts as a horticulturist, Alberta honored him by dedicating a forest reserve the Bugnet Historical Plantation Site. It is an especially appropriate memorial to a man whose love of nature was central to his work.

and award their finest works. Alberta's Department of Culture has even supported an annual "Search for a New Alberta Novelist" competition.

While the performing arts and literature thrive in Alberta, a growing film and television industry also plays an important role in the province's economy and culture.

A Center for Film and Television

As long ago as 1919, the wilderness adventure film *Back to God's Country* established Alberta as a prime filmmaking venue in Canada. The film, starring the groundbreaking actress/director Nell Shipman and shot on location in Lesser Slave Lake in northern Alberta, made a hefty profit for its Calgary investors and sowed the seeds for a successful film industry in the province. Since that time, Alberta's striking landscape and open business climate have made the province a prime location for shooting feature films, television series, and commercials. In a recent year Alberta attracted almost $200 million in investments in film and television production.

The province's diverse settings attract filmmakers from the United States and elsewhere. The bear-attack thriller *The Edge* was shot not in Alaska, its setting in the film, but in Alberta. Parts of other Hollywood feature films, such as *Shanghai Noon* and *Texas Rangers,* have recently been shot in Alberta. In Calgary, the combination of big-city streets and nearby rugged terrain makes ideal filming for commercials for cars, trucks, sportswear, and other products.

A major reason for Alberta's recent success in attracting film and television projects is the newly formed Alberta Film Development Program, which offers millions of dollars worth of incentives every year to local producers. Film companies also find that Alberta—and other Canadian sites, such as Vancouver in British Columbia—have a better film infrastructure than, for example, cities in Alaska.

Calgary has been especially aggressive in establishing itself as a film center. The Calgary Film Services Office effectively promotes the city's unique characteristics to filmmakers. Located in the foothill parklands but within an hour of the Rockies, Calgary makes an ideal location for many feature films and television series. A new "one-stop shop" studio, called CFB Calgary because it was once a Canadian Forces base, is becoming the center of production in the city by providing soundstages, production offices, and an equipment supplier. Calgary is also home to the Quickdraw Animation Society, which promotes animated films by offering scholarships, networking contacts, and member profiles.

Alberta is not only a good spot for outside filmmakers, it has supported efforts to produce home-grown films and television programs. Most notably, the Edmonton-based Alberta Motion Picture Industries Association, made up entirely of Alberta writers, directors, actors, and craftspeople, promotes Alberta films by Albertans, with the goal of portraying Alberta's urban and rural identity to the outside world.

The people of Alberta embrace festivals and the performing arts but it is outdoor recreation and sports such as ice hockey that really capture public attention.

Where Hockey and Football Rule

For the past thirty years, professional ice hockey has been a popular mania in Alberta. The province is home to the National Hockey League's Edmonton Oilers and the Calgary Flames, arch rivals that reflect the friendly competition between the two cities. The Oilers, led by Ontario-born superstar Wayne Gretzky, in the 1980s evolved into one of the most dominant dynasties in recent hockey history. The team won five Stanley Cup Championships between 1984 and 1990. After the first one, the city of Edmonton erupted into a celebration that locals said rivaled that of Victory-in-Europe Day, when Germany conceded defeat during the last months of World War II. The Calgary Flames' history is only slightly less prominent than the Oilers'. The team has advanced twice to the Stanley Cup finals, successfully claiming the 1989 trophy.

The Oilers and the Flames have rabid fans—outsiders can hardly imagine the importance of professional hockey to many residents of Alberta. Former Edmonton resident Deanna Creighton remembers Stanley Cup weeks in which her family had televisions in the basement, the front room, and the

■ *Wayne Gretzky holds the Stanley Cup over his head after leading the Edmonton Oilers to a 1984 victory.*

bedrooms tuned to the championship games. The family had prepared food and appetizers to enjoy throughout the game. Nobody left the house or even answered the phone. When the Oilers scored, the cheers of family members mingled with those from across the street and around the city.

While not as popular as professional hockey, football also has a prominent place in Alberta. Edmonton and Calgary both host Canadian Football League teams: the Eskimos in Edmonton and the Stampeders in Calgary. The Eskimos have claimed eleven Grey Cup Championships in their history and the Stampeders five. The teams enjoy broad support in Alberta. As with ice hockey, the games are cultural markers for Albertans. Many fans remember the greatest events in team history, points in time that help them connect to their teams and to each other.

A Province of Players

Albertans' love of professional sports translates readily into an appreciation of participatory sports and recreation. Hockey, curling, ice-skating, and other activities are important community activities. In many cities, local taxes support public ice rinks. Eric Cook, a former Edmonton resident, recalls frigid days with snow piled higher than his waist. But always, the sidewalks and trails leading to the rinks had been plowed, enabling young skaters and hockey players, no matter what the weather, to play. Thus, recreational hockey has become much like basketball or baseball in the United States—a sport youngsters of all abilities flock to and play anytime.

In addition to hockey, figure skating and speed skating are booming in popularity. Clubs for adults and youths have popped up around Alberta. They attract various participants, from competition-bound youths to adults who enjoy the recreation. The clubs generally offer skating classes at various skill levels.

In addition to hockey and skating, Alberta residents love curling, a sport played by pushing a forty-two-pound polished stone across ice, with broom-wielding sweepers to guide its path. Growing numbers of Albertans find this "chess on ice" appealing at least in part because the game does not require extraordinary athletic prowess. Like ice-skating, curling has spawned numerous community clubs and organizations, many of which compete at amateur levels.

■ Alberta's Gold-Medal Pairs Skaters

At the Salt Lake City Winter Olympics in 2002, Jamie Salé and David Pelletier stole headlines with their flawless pairs skating performance and the controversial silver medal they were awarded the night of the final pairs competition. The two were later awarded duplicate gold medals after an International Skating Union investigation ruled a French judge guilty of misconduct in her scoring.

Even prior to the Olympic headlines, Salé and Pelletier had become the darlings of Alberta. Born in Calgary and raised in Red Deer, Salé began skating before she was even two years old. By age eight she was talking to her mother about making the Olympics. Salé skated singles and pairs growing up, but after focusing on pairs and achieving only moderate success (a twelfth-place finish in the 1994 Olympics pairs), she looked for a new partner and a new focus—and found them in David Pelletier.

Pelletier, raised in Lachine, Quebec, had skated since he was four, though ice hockey rather than figure skating was his first love. Like Salé, he eventually turned to pairs but enjoyed only moderate success with other partners. Both skaters were working other jobs and seemed to be on the verge of leaving behind competitive figure skating in 1998 when Pelletier flew to Edmonton to meet with Salé. The two agreed to rededicate themselves to the sport. Soon after teaming up, they began winning medals. Their success culminated with a victory at the world championships in 2001 and the silver-turned-gold at the 2002 Winter Olympics. The two are also a pair off the ice in Edmonton, where they live together and train. They say they receive constant encouragement from neighbors and friends.

■ *Pelletier and Salé display their silver medals at the 2002 Winter Olympics.*

Love of Outdoors

Beyond community sports, the people of Alberta enjoy their land and take advantage of the mountains, rivers, and woods in a variety of ways. The Banff and Jasper National Parks, in particular, are well known for attracting recreational tourists and outdoor sports enthusiasts. One recent survey showed that an astonishing 72 percent of the residents of Calgary had visited Banff in the previous year.

During the winter, the parks offer a range of recreational opportunities. Skiing and snowboarding enthusiasts pack the lodges in the towns of Banff and Lake Louise in Banff National Park. The slopes nearby are known for their frequent white powder. For those people who do not care for downhill, there are plenty of areas for cross-country skiing and snowshoeing. Winter tourists can opt to snowmobile in the backcountry or, for a fee, follow guides into some of the Rockies' caves. Experienced spelunkers (cave explorers) rappel deep into caves and crawl through twisty passageways, sometimes arriving at underground caverns and pools. Also popular in the winter are dogsledding, sleigh riding, and sightseeing.

Even greater numbers of Albertans—and visitors from other provinces and around the world—head for the mountains in the summer to hike, fish in the mountain streams, and camp. With almost untouched wilderness, huge icefields, and endless trees, the Canadian Rockies make for world-class sightseeing. The scenic Icefields Parkway that bisects Banff and Jasper National Parks is one of the single most popular tourist attractions in Canada.

Alberta's summer adventurers can also kayak or raft through whitewater on the Kicking Horse, Sulphur, or Kakwa Rivers, among others. Travelers to Cold Lake, on the Saskatchewan border 150 miles (240 kilometers) northeast of Edmonton, can find a huge marina for boating as well as good fishing. The nearby Lakeland Provincial Park, in the transition zone from parklands to boreal forest, attracts bird watchers, mountain bikers, kayakers, and nature lovers.

One of Alberta's newest provincial parks, Lakeland joins more than 500 other provincial parks, reserves, and wilderness areas in Alberta. In recent years the province has sought to dramatically expand its total protected acreage and thus increase outdoor recreational opportunities and conserve its wildlife. Exactly how to balance Alberta's exquisite environment, however, with the demands of jobs, resource management, and native land claims remains one of a number of thorny problems for the province.

Facing the Future

W hile oil and natural gas have helped make Alberta wealthy, they have also contributed to some of Alberta's most difficult problems. Alberta's somewhat sudden energy-derived wealth has created resentment in sister provinces. The people of Alberta, in turn, have begun to resent the transfer, through Canadian federal taxation policy, of their province's wealth to poorer parts of the country. In addition, Alberta's wealth has failed to resolve serious problems in the health care system—thousands of people are stuck on waiting lists, and health care costs continue to soar, even while provincial and federal government revenues fall in the face of global economic decline. Thus, Alberta has taken the controversial lead in moving toward a semiprivatized health care system.

Beyond those challenges, the oil, gas, and timber industries are always plagued by environmental concerns. The federal government would like to support international treaties aimed at curbing global warming, but Alberta's energy workers feel that their livelihoods are being threatened. And while the province has risen in general prosperity over the last half-century, the distribution of prosperity has been uneven. Alberta's First Nations and Métis peoples still suffer from debilitating poverty, and many are engaged in lawsuits aimed at securing greater landholdings and increased public support.

Sharing the Energy Wealth

While it is true that Alberta's prosperity has come mainly from the energy industry in the last fifty years, the industry's up-and-down nature has also posed some of the province's most

■ *Environmentalists dressed as dinosaurs protest Alberta's oil industry by placing "environmental tickets" on police cars in downtown Calgary.*

pressing challenges. High oil prices mean that the provincial government earns more from its leases and can keep taxes low—and Alberta is proud of its status as the lowest-taxed province in Canada. But the province relies heavily on its energy revenues. When a worldwide recession causes the demand for oil and gas to fall, provincial revenue can plummet.

Alberta's fortunes can also be impacted by events such as the September 11, 2001, terrorist attacks on the United States. Provincial energy revenues were expected to fall by more than 5 percent in the immediate aftermath of 9/11. This setback occurred at a time, moreover, when revenues from energy industries were already down from the previous year because of a weakened world economy. Meanwhile, the province's costs of health care and children's services continue to rise, leading Alberta to raise insurance premiums, tobacco taxes, and motor vehicle fees to help pay for crucial services. "While Alberta's economy continues to be strong, dramatic drops in the price of oil and gas translate directly into a significant hit on provincial revenues,"[25] remarked Alberta's minister of finance Patricia Nelson.

In addition, the Canadian government uses federal income taxes to make "equalization payments" to the provinces least capable of raising revenues from their citizens to pay for social services. While taxpayers across the country, then pay for the equalization programs, those from more prosperous provinces (in recent years, primarily Alberta, Ontario, and British Columbia) contribute more to the program than they get in return. Their residents end up supporting poorer provinces (lately, mainly Quebec, Manitoba, and the maritime provinces), which received in total about $10 billion per year in equalization payments from 1999 to 2001.

This process worsens already troubled relations between Albertans and their fellow Canadians. Even prior to their entrance into the confederation, Albertans were suspicious of easterners and regarded themselves as tougher and better able to handle the challenges of nature and shifting economies. Today, many Albertans feel that their strengths subsidize the presumed weaknesses of other provinces. Alberta officials have been known to lash out at representatives of other provinces who suggest taxing an even greater share of Alberta's energy revenues.

The rapidly fluctuating energy industries continue to cause other problems for the province. After the 9/11 terrorist attacks, airline travel—and therefore demand for jet

■ Diversifying the Economy

The energy industry has been the engine of Alberta's economy for decades now, but relying too much on it left the province in financial trouble in the mid-1980s and early 1990s. Since that time, the province has worked to increase the influence of other industries—and the effort seems to be paying off. In 1985, 38 percent of Alberta's gross provincial product came from the energy industries. By the end of the 1990s, that number had fallen to 19 percent, in large part because manufacturing industries, like food and timber processing, and business and community services had made significant advances. Now Alberta wants to go to the next level—high-tech.

With no provincial general sales tax, low property taxes, the country's lowest gasoline tax rate, and low personal and corporate income tax rates, Alberta is attractive to new businesses, including high-tech companies. More than fifteen hundred such companies now operate in Alberta, providing more than forty thousand jobs and $9 billion in annual revenue. Technology shipments have grown at an annual rate of almost 15 percent. Worldwide, technology-based industries have suffered in the last few years. But Alberta is predicting continued growth for its economy, in part because of its low tax base and its new high-tech industries.

fuel—plummeted, while a warmer-than-usual winter that year also drove down the price of oil and natural gas. New security measures add to the costs of doing business, both in terms of money and in time spent getting Alberta's goods across the border into the United States. These costs are particularly damaging since exports to the United States make up 25 percent of Alberta's gross provincial product.

But beyond even financial difficulties, the energy industries pose other issues. Albertans treasure their spectacular mountains, forests, rivers, and lakes. But the demands of industry and the energy-driven economy may raise difficult choices in the times ahead.

Limiting Greenhouse Gases

■ *An oil burn-off at a pumping facility near Edmonton produces dangerous and controversial greenhouse gasses.*

Alberta's petroleum industry was at the center of a national debate in recent years. This dispute was over greenhouse gases, pollutants such as carbon dioxide and methane that build up in the earth's atmosphere, potentially causing the earth's climate to heat up. The United Nation's Kyoto Protocol, developed over a number of years in the mid-1990s and gathering signatories since 1998, is an internationally-agreed-upon set of guidelines. The protocol is directed mainly at industrialized nations such as Canada and aims to curb the world's annual production of greenhouse gases. Unlike the U.S. government, which has been critical of the Kyoto Protocol, the Canadian government has generally supported it and as of mid-2002 appeared ready to officially sign the treaty.

Because greenhouse gases are mainly generated by burning fossil fuels such as crude oil, natural gas, and coal, Alberta produces more greenhouse gases than any other province. This has led the petroleum industry in Alberta, as well as the provincial government, to adamantly oppose Canada's willingness to accept strict reductions in greenhouse emissions. Reducing greenhouse gases means Alberta's oil companies would need to develop costly new technologies. A provincial government report released in spring 2002 claimed that the economic fallout of Kyoto could be catastrophic in Alberta, leading to extra costs of up to $5.5 billion a year and the loss of seventy thousand jobs.

Even prior to the debate over whether Canada should sign the Kyoto Protocol, Alberta officials had become aware of the need to reduce greenhouse gases in the province. The provincial government sought to demonstrate leadership through its actions by reducing emissions from government operations. According to a provincial report, "By the end of 1998, actions taken to reduce greenhouse gas emissions associated with Alberta government operations had resulted in a 17.3% reduction in emissions . . . below 1990 levels."[26] The demands of the Kyoto Protocol, of course, would dwarf the impact of what the provincial government does solely within its own operations. Environmentalists in Alberta acknowledge the province has made some progress on the issue. They contend that more must be done, however, arguing that increasing greenhouse gases across the country could cause a human and economic disaster in later decades unparalleled in human history.

As with other issues, the greenhouse gases debate seemed to polarize Alberta and the nation. A Quebec government official suggested that since Alberta produced most of the country's greenhouse gases, it should pay for most of the upgrades needed to reduce emissions. This prompted Alberta's environment minister Lorne Taylor to complain that Quebec, which receives federal equalization payments from provinces such as Alberta, "was in danger of killing 'the goose that laid the golden eggs.'"[27]

Issues Threaten Timber Industry

The future of the timber industry is another pressing concern in Alberta. For both environmental and economic reasons, Alberta's logging industry is now suffering some of its worst times in decades. Prices have fallen dramatically in the last few years, and environmental and trade disputes threaten the future of the industry. Timber has been a mainstay of the provincial economy since 1930. It was then that the passage of the Natural Resources Transfer Agreements (NRTA) gave Alberta and two other provinces, Saskatchewan and Manitoba, control of their own resources and lands.

■ *An aerial view of a forest near Calgary reveals wide swaths of missing growth, the result of clear-cut logging.*

Environmentalists have long contended that loggers were rapidly stripping away Alberta's trees without sufficiently replacing them, thus robbing the province of its natural beauty and of one of its most important resources. When clear-cut logging replaces old-growth forests with plantings of immature trees, environmentalists charge, the new ecosystem seriously disrupts wildlife patterns. For example, environmentalists point to the woodland caribou, which eats the lichen found on old-growth trees and survives against predators by hiding in the deep forests. Rapid deforestation has decreased woodland caribou populations and put the animal on provincial threatened lists.

Alberta's forestry industry also faces serious trade problems. The U.S. government in 2002 threatened to impose protective trade barriers against Canada's timber industry. Regulators in the United States say that provinces like Alberta provide public funds to private logging companies, allowing these companies to charge lower-than-market prices for their timber. This hurts American lumber companies lacking such government support. Canadian and American officials continue to meet to address this issue, but a long-term solution that benefits Alberta's forestry industry seems unlikely.

Alberta's Growing Health Care Crisis

While Albertans enjoy a higher standard of living than many Canadians do, they are finding that the province's energy revenues are not solving the financial issues in the country's public health care system. In 1984, the Canada Health Act revolutionized health care in the country. It declared that health care would be publicly funded, universally available to all Canadians, and comprehensive in its coverage of ailments. Provinces rather than the federal government were given the responsibility to deliver health care and determine how and where it is administered.

In principle, all Canadians are to some degree covered by a basic health care plan, although more options become available under coverages paid into by workers. The arrangement whereby the Canadian government funds health care through the provinces, however, has become increasingly controversial in recent years. Alberta has been among the most vocal critics of the system. In essence, the provinces say that the federal government requires them to provide more health care than the offered funding allows. Services then become rationed not by cost but by time: In many parts of Canada people must wait weeks or even months to see a doctor. Provinces like Alberta have proposed various steps to address this problem. For example, permitting doctors to charge user fees or to bill money for extra services would help to cut down on the overuse problem. The federal government has been adamant, however, that any such provincial schemes would result in reduced health care payments to the province.

■ The Special Places Program

In 1995, Alberta's government unveiled the Special Places program, an initiative to designate more provincial land as parks and reserves and thus protect natural habitats and endangered species. At the time, slightly more than 9 percent of the province was under legislated environmental protection. The bulk of that land, however, was within the five national parks. Over the next five-plus years, Alberta designated 81 new and 31 expanded protected areas covering some 7,700 square miles (20,000 square kilometers), bringing Alberta's total protected area to approximately 12.5 percent of the province.

Environmental activists have generally applauded the program while calling for further reforms to protect threatened species. For example, the province's decision to continue to allow oil and natural gas drilling, logging, and mining on some protected lands has come under fire. Environmentalists also point to the provincial government's own report that large areas of more than 1,500 square miles (4,000 square kilometers) are needed to help populations like the woodland caribou. Most of the province's protected lands are much smaller, although one of the last parks created under the Special Places program, in July 2001, became the province's largest provincially protected area. That is the Caribou Mountains Wildland Provincial Park, which covers 2,300 square miles (6,000 square kilometers) in the woodlands adjacent to the Wood Buffalo National Park. Caribou Mountains contains about 80 percent of the range of at least one population of the threatened woodland caribou.

Under the leadership of straight-talking premier Ralph Klein, Alberta has shown few signs of backing off from a fight with the federal government over health care. Klein has said that key elements of the system must change. He has pointed out that Alberta's health spending recently rose by 80 percent over a six-year period, a rate that is far above the growth in federal funding. Further, many of the newest medical technologies are very expensive, and as Alberta's population ages and needs even more care the system will become increasingly unworkable.

■ *Alberta's premier Ralph Klein (left) shakes hands with the president of the Canada Society.*

A Lonely Position

Opening the door for greater participation by private health care providers has been especially controversial. In 2000, the provincial government passed Bill 11, for the first time allowing the province's private clinics to perform surgeries requiring overnight stays. In 2001 Klein endorsed a provincial task force report that proposed even more sweeping changes. For example, a panel of experts would be set up to determine which services and drugs would be covered in Alberta and which would be removed from coverage. Further, the report advocated setting up health care spending accounts for each individual. Expenses incurred by individuals that exceeded account limits would have to be paid by the individuals.

Opponents of such measures say that they violate the spirit of public health care and could lead to the exclusion of the poor from full medical coverage. The provincial government insists, though, that it "is committed to ensuring Albertans do not have to pay out of their own pockets for health services insured under the Canada Health Act, regardless of where those services are provided."[28] Klein claims that the new policies could ease the tremendous financial obligations borne by the provincial government and could cut down on abuse of the health care system.

In itself, the policy debate further highlights the dramatic ways in which Alberta often sets itself apart from much of the rest of the country. Canadians outside of Alberta worried that the Alberta initiative could set dangerous precedents for the rest of the country. However the health care standoff plays out, it is clear that the province is willing to take innovative—and often lonely—positions on issues of public concern nationwide.

First Nations Land Claims

Health care issues hardly stand alone as a source of bitterness and financial concern within Alberta. The history of the First Nations and Métis peoples continues to haunt the province. Today, aboriginal peoples are asserting their rights with more forcefulness than ever before. The long history of displacement, poverty, and disease has driven aboriginal peoples into the courtroom where, little by little, they are winning battles—and causing divisions within the province.

Treaty 6 in 1876, Treaty 7 in 1877, and Treaty 8 in 1899 between the federal government and various Alberta tribes supposedly ended the land disputes and occasional bloodshed that marked the relationship of the early Canadian government and the Alberta First Nations peoples. Later, the eight Métis settlements set up in the province were meant to settle grievances, as well. Even so, the disputes continue a century later as native land claims prove to be a bitter and volatile issue in Alberta and in the country.

The dispute stems from each party's differing views of the treaties. For most of the past century, courts have upheld the

■ *Prince Charles smokes a peace pipe to commemorate the 1877 treaty between the British government and the Alberta Blackfoot Confederacy.*

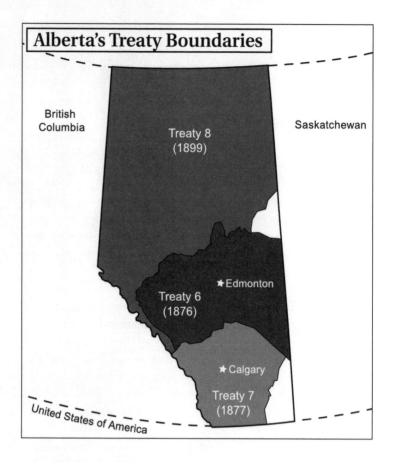

traditional European view—that the treaties gave European settlers certain land rights, set up reservations for aboriginal peoples, and provided cash payouts and education for native peoples. But the First Nations' view of the treaties has always been fundamentally different because of how natives traditionally related to the land, as the following comment from a Canadian-government-sponsored website makes clear:

> The Earth was their Mother, the animals were their spiritual kin and all were part of the greater whole, which was life. Their culture was grounded in nature. . . . While Europeans considered the treaties as transfer of titles to the land, aboriginal nations perceived them merely to be agreements to share the land, as they did with the animals and other groups. While aboriginal people had strong concepts of territory, they did not believe that land was something which an individual could divide, transfer, surrender, destroy or own to the exclusion of others.[29]

In addition, many First Nations peoples have claimed that the Canadian government has continually violated oral promises, made before signing the treaties, to share resources. For most of the past century, Canadian courts held with the government viewpoint. But new Supreme Court rulings such as the surprising Delgamuukw ruling of 1997 have acknowledged the potential validity of aboriginal land claims, and some aboriginal peoples have won rights to pursue fishing and other economic activities on land previously denied them.

Turning to the Courts

Currently, a number of First Nations lawsuits are seeking large financial settlements from the government and Alberta companies, claiming a share of the profits from oil, gas, and other natural resources found on lands aboriginal peoples claim. The Alberta government, meanwhile, maintains that it is fulfilling its constitutional obligations to First Nations peoples and that the 1930 NRTA gave Alberta the authority to administer the resources on public lands. Based on court decisions and land claims, Alberta allows aboriginal groups the right to hunt, fish, and trap on public lands where groups have established title. First Nations peoples see such moves as progress, but claim that they are token actions that gloss over the much larger issue of payment for lands and resources.

■ The Métis Settlements Legislation

In 1990, Alberta became the first province to pass legislation specifically benefiting the Métis people and establishing the only Métis land base in Canada. Alberta also agreed to help set up and fund local councils for Métis self-government. The Métis Settlements Legislation included a series of acts that provides for eight settlements on 2,000 square miles (5,200 square kilometers) of lands. The settlements, mostly located in the transition zone from parklands to forests north of Edmonton, are Buffalo Lake, East Prairie, Elizabeth, Fishing Lake, Gift Lake, Kikino, Paddle Prairie, and Peavine. Approximately six thousand of Alberta's forty-five thousand Métis live on the settlements. Each settlement elects a five-member council that is headed by a chairperson selected by council members. Each council makes bylaws to govern its respective settlement, and the council members belong to the General Council that governs all eight settlements. The legislation also provides for provincial funding of the Métis. In 1998, Alberta spent $12 million to fund the General Council, the settlements, and the Métis Settlements Transition Commission.

■ *Siksika Indians call attention to the land treaties revoked by Alberta's government during their annual protest ride.*

The Alberta government has responded by consulting with First Nations peoples when treaties have been violated in resource development. Further, the government requires developers to undertake historical resources and mitigation studies of cultural sites. The government encourages developers to consult with First Nations peoples in conducting such studies. First Nations peoples, however, say this policy is largely cosmetic, resulting in little real action or compensation.

Finally, according to the NRTA, the Alberta government must provide unoccupied federal land to help the federal government settle its land claims obligations. Alberta officials say that all land claims approved by the federal government have been settled or are being addressed, but the Lubicon Cree of northern Alberta, for one, disagree. The tribe continues to pursue a land claim settlement that they initiated decades ago, while in the meantime a giant multinational company conducts logging operations on the disputed territory. The Lubicon Cree accuse the federal and provincial governments of dragging out negotiations and litigation. Alberta's judges and legislators are likely to stay busy in the near future making difficult decisions on this and other aboriginal land claims.

"Cultural Genocide"

Alberta and its First Nations and Métis peoples are also attempting to come to grips with some ill-conceived social and educational policies that affected thousands of young natives for much of the twentieth century. In 1879, the Canadian government began to set up church-run boarding schools that removed native children from their homes for ten months of the year in order to better assimilate them into white culture. In 1894, the government made attending such schools mandatory. Separated from their parents, families, and communities for much of their lives, many of these young natives grew up alienated, depressed, even suicidal.

Another government policy that evolved in the 1950s seemed to repeat this tragic mistake. Essentially, social workers began to remove thousands of native children from presumably "disadvantaged" homes for foster care or adoption, almost invariably sending these children to nonnatives in distant towns and provinces. This forced removal of one group's children by another group, which a Manitoba judge termed "cultural genocide," was so prevalent during the 1960s that it has come to be called the "Sixties Scoop." By 1969, up to 40 percent of all children in government placement programs were natives, though native peoples made up only 4 percent of the population. Removing native children from their homes was more common in the prairie provinces than elsewhere in Canada.

The long-term effects of these policies, no matter how well intentioned, were disastrous from the point of view of First Nations peoples. Throughout the twentieth century, children not only lost vital months and years away from their homes, they were subjected to physical, emotional, and even sexual abuse. One tragic example is a Métis from northern Alberta who was shipped in and out of numerous foster homes and institutions. "In one," writes Michael Downey, "he was beaten with a stick for wetting the bed. Another provided a bed just two feet wide in a flooded basement. . . . His suicide attempts began when he was 9. At his 16th foster home, aged 17, he nailed a board between two trees and hanged himself."[30]

Only recently has the Canadian government begun to address these issues by forming a commission on the school cases and by considering reparations for the victims of child displacement. In Alberta, provincial officials have taken dramatic steps to reform the child welfare system, creating a child advocate office and mandating that an aboriginal child's

■ *Traditionally dressed Native Canadians playing a round of golf at Banff Springs exemplifies Alberta's unique culture.*

tribal leader and council must be consulted before custody is awarded permanently to anyone. Beyond that, Alberta was the first province to open a Métis-specific child welfare agency, the Métis Child and Family Services of Edmonton. The agency provides foster care placement and emphasizes traditional values when it selects caregivers.

Resolving an Identity Crisis

In sum, much of Alberta has enjoyed great prosperity for many years. But downturns in the world economy regularly threaten that prosperity. At the heart of monetary and energy issues lie, as well, the funding of health care and the safekeeping of the environment. In addition, decades of colonial-type control over its aboriginal peoples have led to persistent social problems. Each of these issues, in some way, poses a threat to the identity of the province as a place where rugged individualists push forever forward with nary a look back. For many of the people of Alberta, however, the building blocks of the future are not only the successes they have enjoyed in overcoming the hardship of life on the plains, but also the prejudices they have confronted. While Albertans struggle to work through these pressing issues, they also work to retain their pride and heritage and yet participate responsibly in the province and in the world.

Facts About Alberta

Government

- Form: Parliamentary system with federal and provincial levels
- Highest official: Premier, who administers provincial legislation and regulations
- Capital: Edmonton
- Entered confederation: September 1, 1905 (same date as Saskatchewan, making the two the eighth and ninth provinces)
- Provincial flag: Alberta's Shield of Arms centered on a blue background
- Motto: *Fortis et Liber* ("Strong and free")

Land

- Area: 255,286 square miles (661,190 square kilometers); 6.6% of total land of Canada; fourth-largest province
- Boundaries: Bounded on the west by British Columbia, on the south by the state of Montana, on the east by Saskatchewan, on the north by the Northwest Territories
- National parks: Banff, Jasper, Wood Buffalo, Waterton Lakes, Elk Island
- Provincial parks: more than 70, plus more than 450 wilderness areas, recreation areas, and ecological reserves,

encompassing approximately 32,000 square miles (83,000 square kilometers)

■ Highest point: Mount Columbia, 12,293 feet (3,747 meters); second-highest peak after Mount Robson in the Canadian Rockies

■ Largest lake: Lake Claire, 554 square miles (1,436 square kilometers), the largest lake entirely in Alberta; Lake Athabasca in Alberta and Saskatchewan is 3,058 square miles (7,920 square kilometers), the 21st-largest lake in the world

■ Other major lakes: Lesser Slave, Utikuma, Bistcho, Cold

■ Longest river: Athabasca, 956 miles (1,538 kilometers)

■ Other major rivers: Peace, North and South Saskatchewan, Slave, Hay, Beaver, Red Deer, Bow

■ Time zone: Mountain Standard Time

■ Geographical extremes: 49°N to 60°N latitude; 110°W to 120°W longitude

Climate

■ Coldest day: –42° F (–41° C) in Coronation on Dec. 19, 1983

■ Longest period of cold weather: 26 days (Jan. 7 to Feb. 2, 1969), temperatures below 0° F (–18° C) in Edmonton (Canadian record)

■ Greatest number of consecutive days with highest temperature above 90° F (32° C): 16, starting July 17, 1925, in Peace River Crossing

People

■ Population: 2,974,807 (2001 census); fourth-highest population of provinces and territories; 9.9% of Canada's total population of 30,007,094

■ Annual growth rate: 10.3% from 1996 to 2001 (highest growth rate among provinces and territories); Calgary accounted for 47% of this growth

■ Density: 11.7 persons per square mile, compared to Canadian national average of 7.8 (4.5 and 3.0 persons per square kilometer)

■ Location: 79.5% urban; 19.5% rural; the Calgary–Edmonton corridor accounts for 72% of Alberta's

population and 7% of Canada's, and includes 6 of the
25 fastest-growing municipalities in Canada

- Predominant heritages: British, French, aboriginal, Métis
- Largest ethnic groups: German, Scandinavian, Russian,
  Chinese, Japanese, Ukrainian, African
- Primary languages (first learned and still understood):
  81% English, 2% French, 17% other led by German,
  Chinese, Ukrainian
- Largest metropolitan areas: Calgary, population 951,395,
  an increase of 15.8% between 1996 and 2001; fifth-largest
  metropolitan area in Canada; Edmonton, 937,845, sixth-
  largest
- Other major cities: Red Deer, Lethbridge, Medicine Hat,
  Grande Prairie, St. Albert, Fort McMurray
- Life expectancy at birth, 3-year average 1995–1997: Men
  75.9 years; women 81.3; total both sexes 78.6, second
  among provinces and territories (Canadian average:
  men 75.4; women 81.2)
- Infant mortality rate, 1996: 6.2 per 1,000 live births,
  ranking seventh among provinces and territories
- Immigration 7/1/2000–6/30/2001: 16,119, 6.4% of
  Canadian total of 252,088; fourth-highest of provinces
  and territories
- Births 7/1/2000–6/30/2001: 35,938
- Deaths 7/1/2000–6/30/2001: 17,508
- Marriages in 1998: 17,651
- Divorces in 1998: 7,668

Plants and Animals
- Provincial bird: Great horned owl
- Provincial flower: Wild rose
- Provincial tree: Lodgepole pine
- Provincial mammal: Rocky Mountain bighorn sheep
- Provincial fish: Bull trout
- Endangered, threatened, or vulnerable species: 41,
  including Banff snail, burrowing owl, bison, whooping
  crane, kangaroo rat, Peary caribou, peregrine falcon,
  polar bear, woodland caribou, trumpeter swan, bull
  trout, ferruginous hawk, northern leopard frog,
  piping plover

Holidays

- National: January 1 (New Year's Day); Good Friday; Easter; Easter Monday; Monday preceding May 25 (Victoria or Dollard Day); July 1 or, if this date falls on a Sunday, July 2 (Canada's birthday); 1st Monday of September (Labour Day); 2nd Monday of October (Thanksgiving); November 11 (Remembrance Day); December 25 (Christmas); December 26 (Boxing Day)
- Provincial: Third Monday in February (Alberta Family Day); 1st Monday in August (optional civic holiday)

Economy

- Gross domestic product per capita: $34,540 in 1999, second among provinces and territories and 102.1% compared to U.S. average[31]
- Gross provincial product: $120.5 billion at market prices in 2000, fourth among the provinces and territories and 11.9% of gross national product
- Oil: world's eighteenth-largest producer; 65% of the country's reserves of conventional crude oil, of which 59% exported to the United States, 25% used within Alberta, 15% used within the rest of Canada, 1% exported overseas
- Natural gas: more than 80% of the natural gas produced in Canada (which is the world's third-largest supplier); Alberta exports about 75% of its production outside the province's boundaries
- Coal: approximately 70% of Canada's reserves and accounts for about half of the country's annual coal production
- Agriculture: wheat, barley, sugar beets, potatoes, dairy
- Tourism: fourth-largest industry, centered around native and western heritage, hiking, sightseeing, skiing
- Logging: pulp, paper, lumber
- Manufacturing: petroleum products, iron and steel, furniture, fiberboard, processed foods and beverages
- Mining: surface materials (sand, gravel); ammonite shell, gold

Notes

Chapter 1: Prairies, Mountains, and Forests

1. Kenneth McNaught, *The Penguin History of Canada.* New York: Penguin, 1988, p. 8.

2. Charles Ora Card, *The Diaries of Charles Ora Card: The Canadian Years 1886–1903.* Donald G. Godfrey and Brigham Y. Card, eds. Salt Lake City: University of Utah Press, 1993, p. 53.

3. Judy Schultz, *Mamie's Children: Three Generations of Prairie Women.* Red Deer, Alberta: Red Deer College Press, 1997, p. 51.

4. Gerald Friesen, *The Canadian Prairies: A History.* Lincoln: University of Nebraska Press, 1984, p. 8.

5. Quoted in Friesen, *The Canadian Prairies,* p. 8.

6. *Bivouac.com,* Canadian Mountain Encyclopedia, Major Ranges, "Rocky Mountains." http://bivouac.com.

7. Andrew H. Malcolm, *The Canadians.* New York: St. Martin's Press, 1985, p. 17.

8. Ray Rasmussen, Alberta's Special Places, "Canadian Shield Region: Alberta, Canada," *Ray's Web Pages.* www.raysweb.net.

9. Rasmussen, *Ray's Web Pages.*

Chapter 2: The Fur Trade and the First Nations

10. *Head-Smashed-In Buffalo Jump,* Blackfoot History, "Social Structure—Basic." www.head-smashed-in.com.

11. *The Provincial Museum of Alberta,* Human History, Archaeology, Aspects of Alberta Archaeology, "Buffalo Hunting in the Alberta Plains." www.pma.edmonton.ab.ca.

12. Richard J. Preston, "The Cree and Métis' Genealogy Page," *The 1999 Canadian Encyclopedia: World Edition.* Toronto: McClelland and Stewart, 1998. *RootsWeb,* Canada, Alberta, "Camrose County." www.rootsweb.com.

13. George Woodcock, *The Hudson's Bay Company.* Toronto: Crowell-Collier, 1970, p. 104.

14. Marcel Giraud, *The Métis in the Canadian West,* vol. I, transl. George Woodcock. Edmonton: University of Alberta, 1986, p. 326

15. Schultz, *Mamie's Children,* pp. 44–45.

16. Schultz, *Mamie's Children,* pp. 45–46.

Chapter 3: Settling the West

17. Pierre Berton, *The Promised Land.* Toronto: McClelland and Stewart, 1984, p. 14.

18. Berton, *The Promised Land,* p. 14.

19. J.G. MacGregor, *North-West of 16.* Rutland, VT: Charles E. Tuttle, 1968, p. 36.

20. *Canada's Digital Collections.* Heritage Community Foundation, Alberta Rural Life, "The Ranch Owners." http://collections.ic.gc.ca.

21. Friesen, *The Canadian Prairies,* p. 239.

22. Berton, *The Promised Land,* p. 255.

Chapter 4: Life in Alberta Today

23. Friesen, *The Canadian Prairies,* p. 427.

Chapter 5: Arts and Culture

24. Berton, *The Promised Land,* p. 278.

Chapter 6: Facing the Future

25. *Government of Alberta,* "Budget Overview." www.gov.ab.ca.

26. *Government of Alberta,* Alberta revenue Business Plan 2001–04, "Environment." www.revenue.gov.ab.ca.

27. Quoted in Brian Bergman, "The Cost of Kyoto," *Maclean's,* March 18, 2002.

28. *Government of Alberta,* News, "Future of Health Care the Subject of Premier's Address," January 21, 2002. www.gov.ab.ca.

29. *Canada's SchoolNet,* First Nations, "Aboriginal Land Claims." www.schoolnet.ca.

30. Michael Downey, "Canada's 'Genocide,'" *Maclean's,* April 26, 1999.

Facts About Alberta

31. *Demographia,* "Canada: Regional Gross Domestic Product Data: 1999." www.demographia.com.

Chronology

ca. 10000 B.C.   Earliest evidence of First Nations settlement in area of present-day Alberta.

ca. 3500 B.C.   Indications of the communal bison hunt, which revolutionized hunting in Alberta.

ca. A.D. 200–1600   Native cultures established societies adapted to the different geographical regions of Alberta.

1670   The Hudson's Bay Company is formed and given the exclusive rights to Rupert's Land, including much of what is now Alberta.

ca. 1720–1730   Earliest indirect contact between natives and Europeans, mostly through trading of furs; arrival of the horse.

1754–1755   Anthony Henday is first European to explore the area on a Hudson's Bay Company trading expedition that travels from York Factory on the Hudson Bay to the North Saskatchewan River.

1778   Peter Pond establishes a trading post south of Lake Athabasca.

1788   The North West Company establishes the first permanent trading post in the area of present-day Alberta, Fort Chipewyan on Lake Athabasca.

1795   The Hudson's Bay Company and the North West Company build forts at the site of present-day Edmonton.

1867 Provinces of Ontario, Quebec, Nova Scotia, and New Brunswick unite to form Dominion of Canada.

1870 Canada purchases Rupert's Land from the Hudson's Bay Company.

1872 The Dominion Land Act draws settlers to the area.

1875 The Northwest Territories Act establishes a government and creates electoral districts; the Northwest Mounted Police build a fort on the site of present-day Calgary.

1876–1877 Canada signs Treaty 6 and Treaty 7 with the Cree, Blackfoot, and other Indian tribes.

1882 Canada carves four administrative districts from the Northwest Territories, including Alberta, named after Queen Victoria's daughter, who is married to Canada's governor general and had just visited the area.

1883 The Canadian Pacific Railway reaches Alberta's eastern border near Medicine Hat; its completion in 1885 increases transcontinental trade.

1897 Gold is discovered in a tributary of the Klondike River in present-day Yukon Territory and sets off a major gold rush; Edmonton claims to be a "Gateway to the North" though ultimately relatively few prospectors leave for the gold fields from it.

1899 Treaty 8 is passed with Cree, Beaver, Chipewyan, and others.

1901 First natural gas well drilled near Medicine Hat.

1905 Alberta and Saskatchewan become provinces and Alberta holds its first elections; in a break from previous cases, the federal government retains rights to these provinces' natural resources.

1906 The first session of the Alberta Legislature confirms Edmonton as the capital and charters the University of Alberta, which opens two years later.

1916   Alberta women get the right to vote in provincial elections.

1919   Railroad workers strike because of poor working conditions, beginning a progressive labor movement in the province.

1930   Canadian law is amended to transfer from the federal to the provincial government all rights to Alberta's minerals and the royalties derived from them.

1930s   Worldwide depression and long-term drought cause many residents to leave the province.

1947   Discovery of oil in Leduc fields near Edmonton sets the stage for economic boom years.

1964   Discovery of the Athabasca River oil sands beds, now recognized as one of the potentially richest oil sands deposits in the world.

1973   Rising oil prices due to OPEC boycott lead to new revenues for Alberta, much of which is funneled into new social programs.

1981   Building begins on the West Edmonton Mall, which later becomes the largest mall in the world and Edmonton's top tourist attraction.

1985   The National Energy Program, begun in 1980 to control oil prices within Canada, is ended, easing tensions between Alberta and other provinces.

1987   Low prices for oil and gas keep provincial economy stagnant, necessitating severe cuts in health care, social services, and education.

1988   Calgary hosts the XVI Winter Olympic Games.

1995   The removal of federally subsidized grain transports leads to the closing of grain elevators and the abandonment of railway tracks throughout Alberta.

For Further Reading

Books

Pierre Berton, *The Last Spike: The Great Railway, 1881 to 1885.* New York: Doubleday, 2002. The prize-winning, best-selling historian tells the stories of Canada's first railroad—the near-bankruptcy of the project, the land booms it triggered, the Chinese workers who helped construct it.

Robert Craig Brown, *The Illustrated History of Canada.* Toronto: Key Porter Books, 2000. With text from seven leading historians, as well as maps, illustrations, and other visual aids, this book takes the reader from Canada's earliest beginnings to the present day.

Don Gillmor, Achille Michaud, Pierre Turgeon, *Canada: A People's History.* Volumes 1 and 2. Toronto: McClelland and Stewart, 2000. A family reference book, the first volume covers the beginnings of Canada to the 1870s while the second volume closes in the 1990s.

Andrew Hempstead, *Alberta and the Northwest Territories Handbook.* Chico, CA: Moon Publications, 1999. This revised third edition provides an excellent description of sights, recreational opportunities, lodging, and more.

Websites

Alberta Heritage (albertaheritage.net). This vast site covers Alberta history, lists youth programs, provides other Alberta heritage and history links, and keeps readers up on Alberta news.

Government of Alberta (www.gov.ab.ca). With links to business, history, environmental, and other subject areas, this site provides extensive coverage of Alberta life.

Works Consulted

Books

Pierre Berton, *The Promised Land*. Toronto: McClelland and Stewart, 1984. Three-time Governor General Award–winner Pierre Berton describes the early settlement policies and immigration patterns that led to the buildup of the Canadian West.

James Blower, *Gold Rush*. New York: American Heritage Press, 1971. This is a useful discussion of the Yukon Gold Rush of 1898 with many pictures from the era.

Charles Ora Card, Donald G. Godfrey and Brigham Y. Card, eds., *The Diaries of Charles Ora Card: The Canadian Years 1886–1903*. Salt Lake City: University of Utah Press, 1993. This lengthy diary of a Mormon pioneer provides a first-hand account of the settling of Cardston, Alberta.

Gerald Friesen, *The Canadian Prairies: A History*. Lincoln: University of Nebraska Press, 1984. This comprehensive history of the western provinces focuses on politics, economics, and major historical events that shaped the West into the 1980s.

Marcel Giraud, *The Métis in the Canadian West*. Vol. 2, Translated by George Woodcock. Edmonton: University of Alberta, 1986. Originally published in 1945, this was the first scholarly examination of Métis history.

Julia D. Harrison, *Métis*. Vancouver: Douglas and McIntyre, 1985. Harrison explores the mixed heritage and complicated history of the Métis of the Canadian West.

J.G. MacGregor, *North-West of 16.* Rutland, VT: Charles E. Tuttle, 1968. This memoir gives a firsthand account of turn-of-the-twentieth-century prairie life.

Andrew H. Malcolm, *The Canadians.* New York: St. Martin's Press, 1985. Malcolm provides a general overview of Canada that leads to a better understanding of the distinct characters of Canadians based on their backgrounds and regions.

Kenneth McNaught, *The Penguin History of Canada.* New York: Penguin, 1988. This is a general overview of major Canadian historical events.

J.H. Paterson, *North America: A Geography of the United States and Canada.* New York: Oxford University Press, 1994. A thoroughly researched discussion of Canadian and U.S. geography that helps readers understand the direct role of geography in regional economies.

Roger E. Riendeau, *A Brief History of Canada.* Allston, MA: Fitzhenry and Whiteside, 2000. A survey of Canada from its earliest inhabitants to today, including many maps and illustrations.

Sara Ellen Roberts, *Alberta Homestead: Chronicle of a Pioneer Family.* Ed. Lathrop E. Roberts. Austin: University of Texas Press, 1971. A pioneer woman who moved with her doctor husband to the Alberta prairies recollects their experiences early in the twentieth century.

Judy Schultz, *Mamie's Children: Three Generations of Prairie Women.* Red Deer, Alberta: Red Deer College Press, 1997. A third-generation prairie woman reflects on the lives and history of her prairie family.

Robin W. Winks, *The Blacks in Canada: A History.* Montreal: McGill-Queen's University Press and New Haven, CT: Yale University Press, 1971. Historian Robin Winks details the long and difficult struggle of blacks entering and living in Canada.

George Woodcock, *The Hudson's Bay Company.* Toronto: Crowell-Collier, 1970. Woodcock explains the turbulent early years of the Hudson's Bay Company and its competitors, describing the competition and violence that led to its merger with the North West Company.

Periodicals and Interviews

Brian Bergman, "The Cost of Kyoto," *Maclean's*, March 18, 2002.

Eric Cook, personal interview, October 20, 2001.

Deanna Creighton, personal interview, October 20, 2001.

Michael Downey, "Canada's 'Genocide,'" *Maclean's*, April 26, 1999.

Internet Sources

Bivouac.com, Canadian Mountain Encyclopedia, Major Ranges, "Rocky Mountains." http://bivouac.com.

Canada's Digital Collections, Heritage Community Foundation, Alberta Rural Life, "The Ranch Owners." http://collections. ic.gc.ca.

Canada's SchoolNet, First Nations, "Aboriginal Land Claims." www.schoolnet.ca.

Demographia, "Canada: Regional Gross Domestic Product Data: 1999." www.demographia.com.

Head-Smashed-In Buffalo Jump, Blackfoot History, "Social Structure—Basic." www.head-smashed-in.com.

Richard J. Preston, "The Cree and Métis' Genealogy Page," *The 1999 Canadian Encyclopedia: World Edition.* Toronto: McClelland and Stewart, 1998. *Rootsweb.com*, Canada, Alberta, "Camrose County." www.rootsweb.com.

The Provincial Museum of Alberta, Human History, Archaeology, Aspects of Alberta Archaeology, "Buffalo Hunting in the Alberta Plains." www.pma.edmonton.ab.ca.

Ray Rasmussen, Alberta's Special Places, "Canadian Shield Region: Alberta, Canada," *Ray's Web Pages*. www.raysweb.net.

Index

Picture Credits

About the Authors

Gordon D. Laws graduated with a B.A. in English from Brigham Young University. He is the author of several short stories, numerous magazine articles, and the novel *My People.* Currently, he is a freelance writer and editor. Lauren M. Laws graduated with a B.A. in history from Brigham Young University. She is a researcher and records expert. This is her first collaboration with Gordon. Gordon and Lauren live in Massachusetts with their son, Grant.